THE ART OF DISTILLING
WHISKEY
AND OTHER SPIRITS

QUARRY

THE ART OF DISTILLING
WHISKEY
AND OTHER SPIRITS

AN ENTHUSIAST'S GUIDE
TO THE ARTISAN DISTILLING
OF POTENT POTABLES

EDITED BY BILL OWENS
AND ALAN DIKTY
FOREWORD BY FRITZ MAYTAG

BEVERLY MASSACHUSETTS

QUARRY BOOKS

First published in the United States of America by

Quarry Books, a member of Quayside Publishing Group
100 Cummings Center
Suite 406-L
Beverly, Massachusetts 01915-6101
Telephone: (978) 282-9590
Fax: (978) 283-2742
www.quarrybooks.com

Library of Congress Cataloging-in-Publication Data

Owens, Bill.
  The art of distilling whiskey and other spirits : an enthusiast's
guide to the artisan distillers of potent potables / edited by Bill
Owens and Alan S. Dikty.
     p. cm.
  Includes index.
  ISBN-13: 978-1-59253-569-9
  ISBN-10: 1-59253-569-0
  1. Distillation. 2. Liquors. 3. Artisans. I. Dikty, Alan S. II.
Title.
  TP156.D5O94 2009
  663'.5—dc22

                                                            2009016457

ISBN-13: 978-1-59253-569-9
ISBN-10: 1-59253-569-0

10 9 8 7 6 5 4 3 2 1

Cover and text design: Don McCartney, Diablo Graphic Design; Walnut Creek, CA

Cover Image: Detail of photo by Andrew Faulkner of a bottle of Prichard's Double
Barreled Bourbon Whiskey
Photo editor: Andrew Faulkner
Illustrations: Catherine Ryan

Photographs: Bill Owens, except: Alan Dikty, page 5; Bill Dowd, page 26; and Andrew Faulkner, pages 7, 8, 9, 11, 19 (center), 29, 39, 40, 41, 42, 43, 44, 45, 46, 48, 49 (top), 52 (center), 54, 55 (top), 57, 58, 65, 66, 69, 70, 75, 77, 78, 81 (left), 83, 84 (top), 85, 88, 89, 90 (left), 91, 93, 95, 97, 98, 101, 102, 103, 104, 105 (left), 106, 107 (top), 108, 112 (bottom), 113, 114 (right), 117 (top right), 129 (top), 144, 147, 148, 152, 153, 159, 163, 164, 165, and 166

Printed in China

DEDICATION

In fond memory of our friend Michael Jackson, who is, we have no doubt, now enjoying his well-deserved angel's share of the world's barrels of maturing whiskey

CONTENTS

FOREWORD

THE SECOND Whiskey Rebellion is happening in the United States, and it is already spreading around the world. In this marvelous book, Bill Owens, Alan Dikty, and their contributors—like intrepid war correspondents—take you to the front lines. You will find here an up-to-the-minute report on the excitement, creativity, and brash enthusiasm of the United States' craft distillers.

Detail of the fermenting process of making bourbon

Charring oak barrels at a cooperage

I have known Bill Owens since his early involvement in the U.S.'s microbrewing renaissance: He was one of the movement's most fervent innovators. His own achievements are many, and his enthusiasm for the whole wild explosion of brewing creativity is evidenced in his obvious enjoyment of the successes of his brewing colleagues.

The craft-brewing renaissance, of course, began in the 1960s. By the early '90s, it was inevitable that it would evolve into a craft-distilling renaissance. And so Bill and his cohorts are at it again, now celebrating a small-distillery revolution and the variety and creativity that is springing up everywhere. Yes, we now have "craft" whiskey distillers, experimenting with all facets of grain distilling. And, as with the brewing revolution, the consumer reaps the rewards. We are entering a golden age for the spirits lover, and *The Art of Distilling Whiskey and Other Spirits: An Enthusiast's Guide to the Artisan Distilling of Potent Potables* is an indispensable guidebook to its beginnings.

Where did the craft-distilling phenomenon originate? You could say that it came down from the mountains, where pot-distilled whiskeys made by hand—in secret folds—have never entirely disappeared. Or you could say that it came up from the vineyards and orchards, where for many years there has been a tiny craft-distilling segment of superb, hand-crafted fruit brandies and eaux-de-vie. Just know that a second

Whiskey Rebellion is upon us and that it is happening right now in a little building near you. And if you have picked up this book already knowing about the great food awakening and hoping for a guide to distilling, you have found it!

What particularly fascinates me about the distillation of alcohol is the enduring mystery surrounding its origins. Distillation itself is a physical art with a long—and colorful—history. And the distilling of all sorts of materials for myriad purposes is an ancient process. But when did the production of distilled spirits as a beverage begin? You are welcome to your opinion, and good luck finding anyone to agree with you! No matter what you think, I encourage you to savor the eternal enigma that is embodied in a distilled spirit. It is a form of magic to take fruit or grain, ferment it, put it in a pot, heat it and make it disappear entirely, and then watch it reappear, drop by drop, as a clear, volatile, almost ethereal liquid. And it is a dangerous liquid—do not kid yourself. It can catch fire, it can explode, and abusing it can ruin lives. It is powerful, mysterious stuff, surely one reason that it captures the imagination of the

producers and consumers swirling and swilling around the current awakening.

So drink deep of Bill and Alan's guide, get on the road with them, go exploring and learning, and enjoy being an early participant in the movement. And take my word for it, as a distiller of whiskey since the second Whiskey Rebellion's first shot: "Heads we win, tails we win!"

Fritz Maytag
Anchor Distilling
San Francisco
April 2009

INTRODUCTION

AS A YOUNG MAN in the 1970s, I had long hair, a Volkswagen Beetle, a hip wife, and a career as a newspaper photographer. I also published four photography monographs, including the classic *SUBUR-BIA* (still in print), and I received a Guggenheim Fellowship in photography and three National Endowment for the Arts grants. My dream was to work for *LIFE* magazine or *National Geographic*, and I ended up stringing for the Associated Press and covered the Hell's Angels beating people with pool cues at Altamont. While all this was happening, I was homebrewing in the garage.

By the 1980s, when I reached middle age, I had a flattop, sold the VW and cameras, and lost a wonderful wife. In 1982, I opened the first brewpub in the United States: Buffalo Bill's Brewery in Hayward, California. The beer was good. My pumpkin ale is still being brewed by many breweries. My public image was "colorful," and the news media loved me. I started believing my own press clips. I opened two more brewpubs and launched a public stock offering to fund the building of a large-scale production brewery. It all seemed like a good idea at the time. It was, after all, "Morning in America," Reagan was in the White House, and the operative phrase for the times was "Greed is good."

I wanted success, money. I had three brewpubs. I grossed a million dollars that year, but I had to pay sixty employees and ended up with no profit. Things don't always work out as you dream. The stock offering never got off the ground, and one by one, the brewpubs were sold off, with Buffalo Bill's being the last to go. But I'll always have Alimony Ale ("The bitterest beer in America!").

By the 1990s, I had gray hair and a new wife, and I was publishing two magazines: *American Brewer* and *BEER: The Magazine*. Once again my timing was good, and the *American Brewer* rode the first great wave of craft brewing. Things were looking great, but financially, the two magazines turned out to be not such a great idea. I soon stopped publishing *BEER* and sold *American Brewer*.

Soon after, the AARP mailings started showing up, and I opened an antique store. That venture lasted six months. Then my agent sold some *SUBURBIA* photographs to Elton John, giving me enough money for a (used) Lexus and the cash for a three-month trip across America, so I ran away from home. On this trip I decided to visit some craft distilleries. I was intrigued, and the creative juices started to flow again. When I returned to California, I founded the American Distilling Institute (ADI). In 2003, I held the first ADI distilling conference at St. George/Hangar One Distillery, and some eighty people showed up.

In 2007, I decided to make another trip across America. Again, the trip was funded by selling photographs to museums, an assortment of art galleries, and friends in the United States and in Europe. This second trip (21,000 miles) took four months, and from fifty-three DVDs of images, we selected a hundred or so for this book. By 2009, the ADI database contained 1,246 names, of which 205 are members, and of those, 165 are craft distillers. The future for the industry is bright. More and more people want to learn the art of craft distilling. They want to learn how to run small businesses selling their handcrafted products to the public. My recent "how-to" book, *Craft Whiskey Distilling*, has sold 300 copies in three months.

The craft distilling industry is really about lifestyle. People take great pride in producing their products. This book is a look at craft distillers and the rest of the whiskey, rum, vodka, and gin industry.

I still have a foot in both camps, photography and distillation. But if I had to choose, it'd be distilling, because it's a way of life.

Special thanks to Alan Dikty, the editor of this book and a personal friend. Alan has been with me as a friend and writer for some thirty years. Alan knows spirits. A big thank-you also to Andrew Faulkner, photographer and photo editor for this book.

Bill Owens
Hayward, California
March 2009

AUTHOR'S NOTE ON SPELLING

For reasons that have yet to be adequately explained, American and Irish distillers spell the word whiskey with an e while their Scotch, Canadian, Japanese, and New Zealand peers spell whisky without it.

CHAPTER ONE

A BRIEF HISTORY OF DISTILLING

SINCE the earliest known use of distillation about 5,000 years ago, practice of the art has grown and spread around the world in several waves, the speed and extent of each being dictated by geography, trade routes, and cultural and religious influences. Each successive wave gave rise to significant technical advances in distillation, making it less expensive, more efficient, and more controllable.

Very Fine Whiskey *bottle, circa the 1920s: This vintage bottle was acquired at a flea market, then filled with Old Forrester.*

Possibly the earliest written record of distillation is in the *Epic of Gilgamesh*, which describes a form of essential oil distillation practiced in Babylon as far back as 3000 BCE. Herbs were placed in a large heated cauldron of boiling water, and the cauldron's opening was covered with a sheepskin, fleece side down. Periodically the sheepskin was changed, and the condensate soaking the fleece was wrung out into a small jar. Essen-tial oils floated to the surface of the water collected in the jar and were skimmed off. Medieval texts and woodcuts show the same principle being used to concen-trate alcoholic vapors from boiling wine. (Incidentally, this is similar in principle to a method that the Phoenicians used for consuming cannabis.)

DISTILLING MIGRATES EAST AND WEST

By 500 BCE, alcohol distillation was an established industry in the ancient Indian area known as Taxila (in modern northwest Pakistan), where archeologists discovered a perfectly preserved terra-cotta distillation system. In this process, steam rising from a pot of boiling water passed through a bed of fermented grains, picking up alcohol and flavors from the grains. The vapors then struck the bottom of a second pot filled with cold water, where they condensed and dripped into a collection tube.

From Taxila, knowledge spread to the East and the West, and by 350 BCE, knowledge of the distilling process appeared in the writing of Aristotle in Greece and Sinedrius in Libya. The first arrival of distillation technology in China is misty, but by 25 CE, bronze stills of similar design were being produced and used there.

By the end of the first millennium CE, the practice of distillation had spread throughout northern Africa and the Middle East. The process had advanced significantly over this thousand-year period, and the material being distilled was now boiled directly in a large sealed pot, which had a long tube leading from its apex to a small collection jar. When the Moors invaded Spain, they brought this technology with them, and soon the genie (or spirit) was out of the bottle. The technology spread from Spain to Italy in 1100 CE, and was recorded in Ireland by 1200, Germany by 1250, and France by 1300. England, Scotland, Poland, Russia, and Sweden joined the club by 1400.

DISTILLING TECHNOLOGY EVOLVES

European exploration and conquest spread rapidly around the world, carrying the technology of distillation with it. The first stills in the Americas appeared not long after the conquistadores, and the Portuguese brought the technology to Japan by 1500.

This technology was largely controlled by alchemists and monasteries, who continuously experimented and improved on the equipment. By the mid-1600s, several texts had been published on the subject of distillation, a sample of which included the woodcuts on this spread, from *The Art of Distillation* by Jonathan French (1651). As this information spread beyond clerical and scientific circles, wealthy individuals began to establish still houses on their estates.

As knowledge blossomed throughout the Renaissance, distillation continued to develop rapidly. Distillation was removed from the exclusive province of scientists, monks, and professionals and became a common household art. Recipe books abounded.

By the 1700s, the complexity and sophistication of commercial-scale distilling equipment advanced rapidly. Advances in the understanding of how distillation actually worked led to new still designs that could make better quality spirits more easily and

*These woodcuts from **The Art of Distillation** by Jonathan French (1651) show a small part of the wide variety of forms distilling equipment had taken by the seventeenth century. Two key improvements are shown: multiple distillations in one setup (one still feeding into the next) top of page, and an improved vapor condenser (a coil of tubing known as a "worm" in a barrel of cold water), below and opposite page.*

"There is more refreshment and stimulation in a nap, even of the briefest, than in all the alcohol ever distilled."

— **Ovid** *(ancient Roman classical poet and notorious wet blanket at bacchanals, 43–17 BCE)*

GEORGE WASHINGTON AND GERRYMANDERING

It is well known that George Washington was a distiller. What is less well known is that the laws he crafted set the distinction between the heavily taxed small distillers and the lightly taxed large distillers, the line being drawn just below the size of his distillery. Politics worked in much the same way then as it does today.

*The George Washington still recreation at the **Mount Vernon Distillery** in Mount Vernon, Virginia*

faster than in the past. Distilling became more accessible to the masses, and the monopoly held by the church and the elite classes was threatened. These centers of power soon enacted restrictions, at first to protect that monopoly, and later purely for revenue.

REGULATION AND REBELLION

Since 1700, the regulation and control of distillation has been mostly a story of lost freedoms and rights. A few rays of sunshine have since poked through the clouds.

The elite and governments of Europe tried repeatedly to exploit and control distillation. In England, for example, the first taxation of commercial distillation appeared in 1690 to pay for a war with France. Private distillation was exempted from this tax, and it remained free from interference as taxes and regulations were raised, lowered, abolished, and resurrected over the next century. Private distillation in England flourished and grew significantly during this time (and perhaps not a little of this product found its way into commercial channels via the back door), until it was outlawed in 1781 to enhance the collection of revenue. The massive Gin Craze of early eighteenth-century Great Britain had its roots, in part, in this unfettered spread of distillation.

Blueprint of a Simple Still

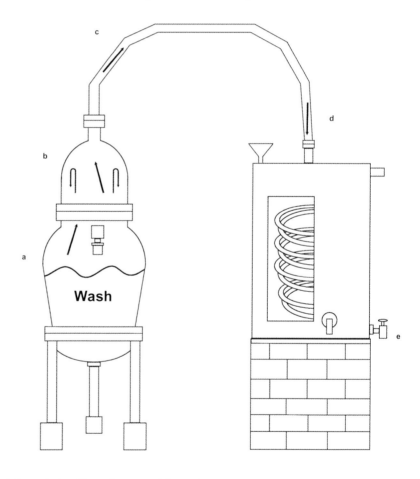

a) *Steam jacket: Heats the pot and the wash*
b) *Pot: Holds the wash*
c) *Swan Neck: Allows for separation of the components of the mixture*
d) *Tube in Shell Condenser: Condenses the alcohol vapors in spirits*
e) *Spigot: The vapors are collected from a spigot at the bottom of the condenser.*

The United States government's first attempt to tax distillation resulted in the Whiskey Rebellion of 1791, which was put down by federal troops led by George Washington (who was brought out of retirement for the conflict).

Federal excise taxes were abolished after the end of the War of 1812, only to be imposed during the Civil War in the 1860s (and continue to this day).

Napoleon introduced regulation in France. The laws varied widely over the next century, but stabilized in 1914, when the right was granted to anyone with a vineyard or orchard to distill up to 20 liters of spirits from their fruit if they agreed to pay a tax. This right was originally inheritable, but that was revoked in the 1950s. This system led to the development of traveling stills, known as *bouilleurs de cru*, which were once very common sights in the French countryside. Because the number of permitted individuals has shrunk with every passing year, very few of these mobile distilleries remain.

Australians lost their right to distill their own beverages in the aftermath of World War I, again as a revenue measure.

Many African, Latin American, and southern European nations have continued to allow private distillation under a wide variety of rules, ranging from none, through inspection of stills, to onerous regulations and high taxation. In general, traditional alcoholic beverages are made in most farmhouses using traditional equipment (mostly pot stills of various forms), without any adverse effects on society.

The most recent and hopeful change in the global regulation of distillation was the legalization of private, noncommercial distilling by New Zealand in 1996. The New Zealand government found that the expense of enforcing the ban on private distillation far outweighed the revenue coming from fines, so the law was abolished. This change led to widespread adoption of small-scale distilling as a hobby, and, as hobbyists always will, they experimented with equipment and techniques continuously. Many significant innovations have been developed, making small-scale distilling equipment more available, much less expensive, and very much easier to control than anything that came before.

FUTURE TRENDS

Just as the appearance of microbreweries followed the renaissance of homebrewing, increasing the choices and level of quality for all beer drinkers, microdistilleries are starting to thrive around the world, some using traditional equipment, but many using new equipment, methods, and techniques developed by the newly liberated home distillers. Many of these modern small distilleries are experimenting with new types and categories of spirits, creating novel and sometimes uniquely local spirits.

MOONSHINE

As surely as thunder follows lightning, whiskey follows beer, and in the 1980s, the scent of whiskey charged the air like an approaching storm

THE PROSPECT of making whiskey, gin, rye, brandy, and other flavorsome spirits at home is enough to make some modern cocktail enthusiasts and craft brewers grow glint-eyed. Ever so quietly, the more adventuresome of them have begun tending home-sized stills to make the smallest-batch American spirits since the Prohibition days of stove-top alky cookers. Unlike unscrupulous producers who made rotgut that could blind, cripple, and occasionally kill its drinkers, many of today's home

Moonshine still, dismantled

A tombstone that was used during Prohibition for stashing moonshine near Morgantown, West Virginia

distillers have adopted high-tech equipment and a code of honor that ostracizes those who try to sell their makings. Because these distillers are running the very best they can for their immediate friends and families, the results can be spectacularly good.

The ability to create personal stocks of liquor from scratch falls squarely in the modern mixologist's pursuit of making what can't easily be had—real grenadine from actual pomegranates; ginger-spiked falernum; Jamaica's pimento dram, a sucker punch of allspice and rum; and potent aromatic house bitters—but all tuned to their personal tastes. When it comes to making the base spirits for those bitters, it couldn't be easier—or cheaper.

BUT IS IT LEGAL?

Making bitters and falernum from pre-distilled spirits is **entirely legal**. However, unlicensed distillers operating unregistered stills violate a number of federal, state, and local laws, but a lack of permits hasn't stopped would-be distillers from buying and building personal stills in increasing numbers since the mid-1990s. Some of them are content with very smooth vodka, while others embrace the entire concept of artisanal production and are creating fantastic small-batch spirits using the best ingredients they can afford. Running these tiny batches, with yields of just a few liters, is a practice some have called *nano-distilling*.

DIRT TRACK DISTILLING

Students of American popular culture know that moonshine whiskey and NASCAR go together like actor Burt Reynolds and muscle cars. Starting in 1973 with the movie **White Lightning**, Reynolds made a career of portraying Southern good ol' boys delivering moonshine in fast cars, while outrunning the local sheriff.

The real-life inspiration for such cinema characters was Robert Glen Johnson Jr. (born in 1931 in Wilkes County, North Carolina), better known as Junior Johnson. Johnson was a moonshiner in the rural South who became one of the early superstars of NASCAR in the 1950s and '60s.

Johnson grew up on a farm and developed his driving skills running moonshine as a young man. He consistently outran and outwitted local police and federal agents in auto chases, and he was never caught while delivering moonshine to customers. Johnson became something of a legend in the rural South, where his driving expertise and "outlaw" image were much admired.

Johnson is credited with inventing the "bootleg turn," in which a driver escapes a pursuer by sharply putting his speeding car into a 180-degree turn on the highway, then speeding off in the opposite direction before his pursuer can turn around. Johnson was also known to use police lights and sirens to fool police roadblocks into thinking that he was a fellow policeman; upon hearing his approach, the police would quickly remove the roadblocks, allowing Johnson to escape with his moonshine.

In 1955, Johnson decided to give up delivering moonshine for the more lucrative (and legal) career of being a NASCAR driver.

Unfortunately, the "Revenues" had not forgotten Junior. In 1956, federal agents found Johnson working at his father's moonshine still and arrested him. Johnson was convicted of moonshining and was sent to federal prison, where he served eleven months of a two-year sentence. He returned to the NASCAR scene in 1958 and picked up where he left off. He went on to win fifty NASCAR races in his career before retiring in 1966.

In 1965, writer Tom Wolfe wrote an article about Johnson in Esquire magazine. The article, originally titled "Great Balls of Fire," turned Johnson into a national celebrity and led to fame beyond

*A POS card advertising **Junior Johnson's Midnight Moon** by **Piedmont Distillers***

his circle of NASCAR fans. In turn, the article was made into a 1973 movie based on Johnson's career as a driver and moonshiner titled The Last American Hero. Jeff Bridges starred as the somewhat fictionalized version of Johnson, and Johnson himself served as technical advisor for the film.

More recently, Johnson's family has licensed the Junior Johnson name for use in promoting a legal distilled product: Junior Johnson's Midnight Moon from Piedmont Distillers in Madison, North Carolina.

A postcard from **Templeton Rye** "Prohibition Era Whiskey"

Label for **Mountain Moonshine** by **Mystic Mountain Distillery**

DON'T TRY THIS AT HOME
(Nudge, Nudge, Wink, Wink, Say No More)

Soon after national Prohibition began in the 1920s, a person could walk into virtually any grocery store in the United States and find for sale brick-size blocks of compressed raisins bound together with condensed grape juice. Attached to the block was a small container of dried yeast. The wrapping contained the following text:

WARNING
Do not dissolve this fruit brick in warm water and then add the contents of the yeast packet, as this will result in fermentation and the creation of alcohol, the production of which is illegal.

Needless to say, the local A&P sold a lot of fruit bricks while Prohibition was in force.

Traditional moonshine starts out with the production and fermentation of what is basically a simple beer. Traditionalists would create a mash of ground corn, hot water, and enough malted barley to provide sufficient enzymes to convert the starch in the grains into simple sugars. Once the starch conver-

sion was complete, yeast was added to the mash, with the resulting fermentation turning the sugars into alcohol. The fermented mash would then be boiled in the pot still to distill off the alcohol.

Alas, times, and moonshine, are not what they used to be. Modern moonshiners tend to skip the grain mashing and go directly to fermentation by dissolving regular sugar in warm water, fermenting the sugar water with baker's yeast, and then distilling off the resulting alcohol. The results are spirit much inferior to a distilled grain spirit, and ultimately an arrested moonshiner. The Alcohol and Tobacco Tax and Trade Bureau (TTB, also known as "the Feds") keeps track of the sale of large quantities of bulk sugar, particularly in rural areas with a past history of moonshining.

You have been warned.

Whiskey is what beer wants to be when it grows up.

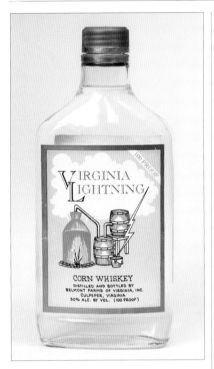

Virginia Lightning Corn Whiskey by **Belmont Farm**

Despite an uptick in amateur distilling and a greater willingness among some to talk more openly about the craft, the long history of secretive, and sometimes violent, moonshining means that, until recently, reliable information was scarce and difficult to verify. That situation is rapidly changing, and distillers, from curious novices to accomplished home artisans, are far from isolated anymore. In less than a generation, they've learned to talk to each other, pool their knowledge, and ask ever more nuanced questions about building and operating a range of stills.

MODERN "MOONSHINERS"

The current interest among hobbyist distillers in creating first-rate liquors, and the general wholesome quality of their products tracks primarily to three convergent trends:

1) Craft brewers
2) New Zealand
3) The Internet

CRAFT BREWERS

Craft brewers are not simply the first ones to study how to make outstanding small-batch spirits; they are also going to shape the face of micro- and personal distilling. Brewers have already mastered three key skills: how to collaborate, how to organize, and how to drive legislation.

The current interest in distilling among brewers is so widespread that it is virtually impossible to talk to craft brewers who aren't already distilling on the sly or working on permits, or know someone who is. One erstwhile brewer framed his transition from beer to liquor with this aphorism: *Whiskey is what beer wants to be when it grows up.*

Chuck Miller *stands in front of his pot still at* **Belmont Farm Distillery**, *one of a dozen distilleries in the United Stated producing a legal moonshine product.*

Making beer at home has been going on for most of the twentieth century, but it's only been legal on a federal level since 1978. For a decade or so after it was permitted, homebrewers (in the United States) explored all kinds of beer and ale styles they could not purchase through their local stores. They perfected their techniques, competed against each other in regional and national contests, published their personal recipes, gave out awards to their peers, and later put that knowledge to use by opening brewpubs and microbreweries everywhere.

Homebrew supply shops everywhere were selling hops, malts, specialty grains, carboys, esoteric scientific equipment, and lab-cultured yeasts to tens of thousands of homebrewers trying, good-naturedly, to best each other in rounds of *My Beer Is Better Than Yours*.

By the 1990s, some brewers were pushing the limits of their equipment and ingredients, becoming essentially novice distillers. Their homemade rigs looked pretty much the same as brewing equipment. The ingredients were the same. They were learning on pot stills because, for hundreds of years, variations on that model had been the choice of folk distilling. Most of what a casual researcher found in popular culture references were the big, copper, pumpkin-shaped boilers of a style that would have been familiar to eighteenth-century farmers.

As brewers, they already knew about grains, malt, yeast, enzymes, ideal fermentation temperatures, filtration systems, and the water profiles that lead to great-tasting beverages. Some had come to believe that the only thing stopping them from having whiskey was too much water. Because they had developed widespread networks for sharing information already—books, magazines, contests, clubs, festivals, newsletters, and rudimentary online newsgroups—questions began to circulate about how best to remove that excess water.

Sharing, critiquing, and judging were an entrenched part of the culture that was starting to take up what had long been a secret practice. Anonymous online forums were ideal tools for vetting home-distilling questions. Unlike the old Appalachian moonshiners, modern distillers with homebrewing backgrounds were already used to talking to each other online and in person.

NEW ZEALAND

Because few of the twentieth-century books on moonshining held much practical information on techniques for building and operating stills, amateur distillers without a family history in such matters learned by trial and

A copper still from **CopperMoonshineStills.com**, *(as seen in the movie* The Dukes of Hazzard*)*

error. Then, in 1996, New Zealand lawmakers scrapped legislation forbidding home distillation. In Australasia, an explosion of interest and innovation, specifically around design for home-size stills that veered off from traditional styles, reverberated widely.

Local distilling enthusiasts were studying the physics of stills, attaching probes and meters to measure exactly what was going on when they fired up. They learned how tall and wide home-size stills should be. They affixed columns to their pots and loosely filled them with ceramic and copper packing material for maximum efficiency. Those stills started looking like something out of a refinery, churning out high-proof alcohol on single runs rather than the multistage process that traditional pot stills called for.

The Internet

These innovative distillers went online and, because their hobby was legal, started talking to each other openly. Brewers who were getting into distilling, with their already established networks and culture of openness, noticed. They seized on a wealth of new verifiable information coming out of the Southern Hemisphere and added their own experiences, especially in online forums.

Since then, as reliable information has been vetted online about how best to build and operate small-scale stills, home column, or reflux, stills have evolved, becoming more compact and efficient, and able to put out as close to

pure alcohol as is possible outside a laboratory (in short, very clean stuff). Most recently, a specific style of distilling has evolved that's all about purity, efficiency, and making lots of neutral spirits in very compact column stills. Easily built and easily operated, they are more efficient and less work than pot stills.

Moonshine Defined

A broad definition of *moonshine* is any liquor made from unregistered stills by unlicensed distillers. This definition covers a Kentucky farmer making the liquor his father did, a New York imbiber wresting 10 ounces of gin from a case of Budweiser, as well as a San Francisco chef tweaking her grandmother's kümmel to carry on the tradition.

Today's nano-distillers don't sell their products. In fact, profit seems almost anathema. One of the quickest ways to really anger others is for unlicensed distillers

to start selling their makings. Some embrace the moonshiner identity; others avoid the term because of its association with lawlessness.

Regardless of what distillers call themselves, they fall into three loose categories—**economic**, **technical**, and **artisanal producers**.

Economic distillers

Economic distillers make liquor because homemade is cheaper than store-bought. Any type of still might be used, from an inherited copper pot still, to modern reflux models, or even an aquarium heater in a plastic bucket. They are apt to distill sugar spirits, but also grains and fruits when they may be had inexpensively. Although their products are prone to be of questionable quality, they are not necessarily bad liquor—think of marc and grappa, made from pomace that might otherwise be thrown away.

Technical distillers

Technical distillers are armchair (or even professional) engineers and chemists, gearheads who strive to make the most efficient distillery setup they can, forever tweaking and adjusting their rigs, creating technological wonders. They run and rerun a batch of spirits to create the purest spirit they can, taking meticulous notes of every temperature fluctuation, proof variation, and yield. Technical distillers tend to have an inordinate amount of vodka on hand because the end result of their frequent experiments is often

Fig. A: Diagram of a Column Distiller

Illustration from *Whiskey: Technology, Production, and Marketing*. Edited by Inge Russell. Academic Press, 2003.

Condenser

Reflux

Water

Distillate

Rectifying section

Column

Stripping section

Reboiler

Steam

Residue

Fig. B: Dimensions of a Typical Spirits Still

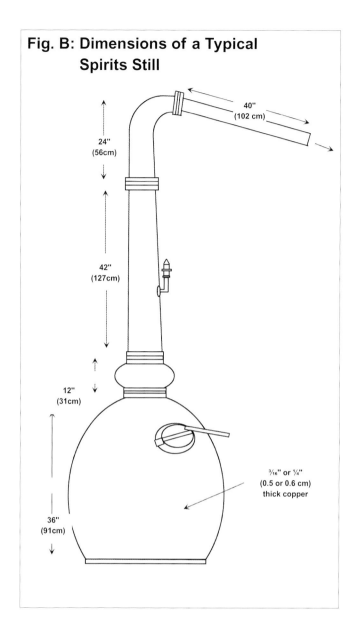

24" (56cm)

40" (102 cm)

42" (127cm)

12" (31cm)

36" (91cm)

³⁄₁₆" or ¼" (0.5 or 0.6 cm) thick copper

---

a high-proof, nearly pure spirit they can supplement with extracts and essences for the exact flavor they want.

ASPIRING AND ACCOMPLISHED ARTISANS

Aspiring and accomplished artisans comprise the third group, whose goal is to make authentic and great-tasting spirits. While technical distillers consider

unwanted chemical compounds obstacles to pure liquor, artisans rightfully regard taste and aroma as the backbone that defines their own personal style of distilling. They tend to use less-efficient, old-school pot stills—they might immediately recognize the kind that a farmer used in 1740. Some use column stills, but without the columns at maximum efficiency, thus preserving taste and aroma

by not distilling to the highest proof possible. Finally, they tend to ferment grains and fruits rather than sugar, and not to care what it costs—because it's for them, not for sellin'.

Fig. C: Anatomy of a Pot Still

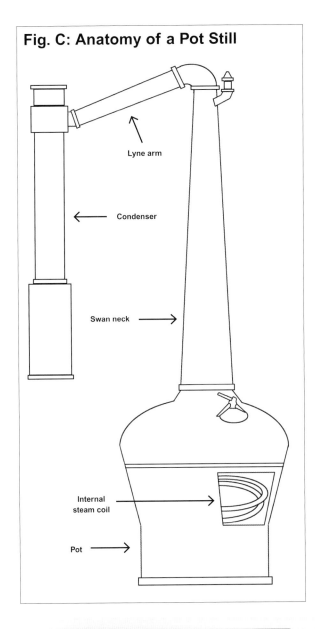

Lyne arm

Condenser

Swan neck

Internal
steam coil

Pot

Fig. A: This flowchart illustrates how the wash is transformed into spirits. The bottom of the still strips out the water, while the rectifying section (top of the still) distills the liquors to increase their spirituosity.

Fig. B: A pot is wider than tall, allowing vapors to escape from the wash. A tall swan neck allows for separation of the components of the mixture. The shape of the still affects the flavor components of the spirits. Every pot still is unique, as distillers want distinctive flavor profiles in their finished spirits.

Fig. C: As illustrated here, a whiskey still has four parts: pot, swan neck, lyne arm, and condenser. The shape of each affects rectification and the flavor of the spirit.
Pot: The pot can by any shape: round, onion, or conical. The shape of the pot affects how the wash is heated (always to 172°F [78°C]). It can be heated by direct fire, steam, gas, or wood. Most pots have a sight glass so the distiller can check for foaming during the distillation process.
Swan neck: The swan neck sits on top of the pot. It can be tall, short, straight, or tapered. Often the swan neck is connected to the pot via an ogee, a bubble-shaped chamber. The ogee allows the distillate to expand, condense, and fall back into the pot during distillation. Most pot stills have a tapered swan neck, allowing for better separation and better enriching of the spirits during distilling.
Lyne arm: The lyne arm sits on top of the swan neck. It can be tilted up or down, and it can be tapered or straight. Often pot stills are fitted with a dephlegmator, or a purifier. Its main purpose is the enrichment of spirits before they're sent on to the condenser.
Internal steam coil: The internal steam coil heats the wash to 173°F (78°C), where the alcohol separates from the wash.
Condenser: The condenser, or worm, is used for cooling the spirits and providing a small stream to a collection tank or pail.

ECONOMICAL INGREDIENTS FOR DISTILLING

Consider a glut of plums for backyard slivovitz, or a skid of dried fruit at bargain pricing that can be turned into Arabian siddiqui. However, ersatz whiskeys made from breakfast cereals are not unheard of, so caveat emptor is the rule.

A fruit eau de vie fermentation at **Stringer's Orchard Wild Plum Winery & Distillery**

CHAPTER TWO

THE DISTILLING PROCESS

IN THE MOST literal sense of the word, distillation means the concentration of the essence of a substance by separating it from any other substances that it is mixed with. In the case of distilling alcohol, this means boiling a fermented liquid in a still to separate the ethanol from the solids, water, and other chemical compounds in the fermented solution. But just as the devil is in the details, the art of distilling is in how the distiller achieves that separation, and how precise that separation is.

The wide range of stills described in this chapter each originally evolved to meet the requirements of producing a particular type of spirit. Depending on the type of spirit being made, precision is not necessarily the goal of the distiller. Thousands of chemical compounds are created by fermentation and distillation, all of which can have, for better or worse, an effect on the ultimate taste or character of a distilled spirit. The distiller's primary job is to retain the desired flavor elements, while discarding those that are not. This is not as simple as it sounds. And despite all of the high-tech controls in a modern distillery, the still master nevertheless has the final call.

The condenser cools the vapors into liquid spirit, which is collected and bottled.

> *"Glass of brandy and water! That is the current but not the appropriate name: ask for a glass of liquid fire and distilled damnation."*
>
> —Robert Hall, nineteenth-century temperance crusader who was never the life of the party

HOW DISTILLATION WORKS

Distillation is a physical process in which compounds are separated by virtue of their different boiling points. Two compounds with the same boiling point occurring together would not be separable by distillation. Fortunately, such occurrences with the ingredients in liquor and spirits are rare.

The separation in distillation occurs when a mixture of compounds in the still is brought to a boil. Compounds with lower boiling points vaporize at lower temperatures than compounds with higher boiling points. This means that the vapor, or steam, rising off the boiling mixture is richer in the lower-boiling-point compounds than in the higher-boiling-point ones. Next, this vapor is collected and cooled to condense it back into a liquid. The resulting liquid, called the **distillate**, contains a considerably higher concentration of the lower-boiling-point compounds than of the higher-boiling-point ones.

In a simplified example, let's consider a mixture of 90 percent water and 10 percent ethanol. Water has a boiling point of 212°F (100°C), and ethanol has a boiling point of 173.1°F (78.4°C). The ethanol will boil and vaporize well before the water, so when the vapors are collected and condensed, the resulting distillate will have a high concentration of ethanol and comparatively little water. The distillate will not be pure ethanol because some water will vaporize at the boiling point of ethanol, even if the water itself is not at its boiling point.

Tails (see page 36) start at 203°F (95°C) and contain a high percentage of fusel oils, known to distillers as wet dog bouquet. A little bit is actually needed in some types of whiskey, but only a little bit. Think Islay Scotch Whisky.

Because all the compounds in a still will vaporize to a greater or lesser extent during boiling, the separation of the compounds will not be perfect, so more elaborate stills have been developed to intensify the separation of the vapors once they have left the boiler. In modern high-separation stills, this is done by employing a reflux column to manage the vapors after they leave the boiler and before they are condensed and drawn from the still.

A STILL'S BLUEPRINT

The whiskey still has four parts: pot, swan neck, lyne arm, and condenser. The shape of each section affects rectification (redistillation) and the taste of the spirits. There is no perfect design; each manufacturer says its pot still makes the best-tasting whiskey.

At this point, distilling is an "art." To make good whiskey, you need to have good ingredients (clean wash) and a good palate (nose and tongue), and you need to know when to start and stop (making head and tail cuts). When it comes to whiskey distilling, the process is controlled by a distiller, not a computer or a manual.

The **pot** can be any shape: round, onion, or conical. The shape of the pot affects how the wash is heated (to 172°F [77.8°C]). It can be heated by direct fire, steam, gas, or wood. All systems have advantages and disadvantages. There is no right way to heat wash. Most manufacturers, however, prefer a double-jacketed steam-water system that provides a gentle heat to the wash. Mainly, you don't want to burn the wash. Most pots have a sight glass so

WHAT A DIFFERENCE A DEGREE MAKES

Between 174° (78.8°C) and 175°F (79.4°C) a veritable witch's brew of nasty chemical compounds (known collectively as heads) are cut and removed by proper distilling. These include acetone, aldehydes, and methanol. Lazy moonshiners tend to leave them in, resulting in rotgut and a serious head-banging headache the next morning as you lie in bed and pray for the Angel of Death to come and finish the job.

THE CHEMISTRY OF PURE SPIRITS

Even a modern high-separation still cannot produce pure ethanol. This is because water forms an azeotrope with ethanol. An azeotrope is a mixture of two liquid compounds whose molecules become loosely bonded such that they have a common boiling point that is different from either constituent's. In the case of ethanol and water, the **azeotrope** *occurs at a mixture of 96.5 percent ethanol and 3.5 percent water, and it has a boiling point of 172.67°F (78.15°C). This is 0.45°F (0.17°C) lower than the 173.12°F (78.4°C) boiling point of pure ethanol. In distillation, this azeotrope is a single compound with a boiling point of 172.67°F (78.15°C), and the still proceeds to separate it on that basis. The ethanol that is purified by a fractionating column is not, therefore, pure 100 percent ethanol but pure 96.5 percent ethanol, with the "impurity" being pure water. No amount of redistillation under the conditions discussed here will influence this percentage; 96.5 percent alcohol by volume (ABV) is the theoretical maximum purity that can be derived by the above process.*

The temperatures stated above are at standard atmospheric pressure. In a column still, due to increased pressure at the bottom resulting from the pressure drop over the plates, the temperatures would be quite a bit higher than stated. For example, the spent wash, which would have a boiling point of about 212°F (100°C) at standard pressure, would have a boiling point of about 220°F (104.4°C) due to the increased pressure.

the distiller can check for foaming during the distillation process.

The **swan neck** sits on top of the pot. It can be tall, short, straight, or tapered. Often the swan neck is connected to the pot via an ogee, a bubble-shaped chamber. The ogee allows the distillate to expand, condense, and fall back into the pot during distillation. Most pot stills have a tapered swan neck, allowing for better separation and better enriching of the spirits during distilling.

The **lyne arm** sits on top of the swan neck. It can be tilted up or down, and it can be tapered or straight. Most arms are tapered down. Often pot stills are fitted with a dephlegmator, or what Scottish distillers call a purifier. The dephlegmator is fitted with baffles that use water plates or tubes to cool the distillate, sending 90 percent of it back into the pot. Its main purpose is the enrichment of the spirits before they're sent on to the condenser.

The **condenser**, or **worm**, is used for cooling the spirits and providing a small stream to a collection tank or pail.

A small pot still, similar to many moonshine stills, is in operation for tourists to see at the Glenmorangie Distillery, Scotland.

WHISKEY STILLS IN DETAIL

There are several different designs of stills used for making whiskey. These include the moonshine still, gooseneck still, continuous-run column still, French Charentais alambic still, and artisan pot still. (The traditional English spelling of this French word is *alembic*.)

MOONSHINE STILL

The most basic and rudimentary design is a crude pot still, or moonshine still, which is a closed pot, like a pressure cooker, with a pipe leading from the lid into a condenser coil. The condenser coil can either be long enough to air-cool the vapors, or it can be shorter and immersed in a water jacket. Such a still affords minimum separation of the vapors because there is almost no separation once they leave the boiler. Although this design of still is not suitable for producing beverage alcohol by modern standards, it will still concentrate an 8 or 10 percent ABV wash to 60 percent in a fairly fast run.

There are many home distillers and illicit commercial moonshiners using this type of still today. And, because this type of still is typically heated on a stove top or on a gas burner, it is necessary to remove all suspended solids from the wash before placing it in the boiling pot. To do otherwise would risk burning solids on the bottom of the pot.

Fig. A: In the basic moonshine still, vapors from the heated wash rise into the cap.

After hitting the flat top of the still, vapors exit via the lyne arm into the condenser, where they condense and become spirits.

Fig. B: The bubble caps sit on tray over vapors tubes in the column. The caps provide contact between the rising vapors and descending reflux, creating a distilling cycle and enriching the alcohol. Arrows indicate vapors rising from the wash and hitting the bubble caps. A percentage of pure vapors continue to rise and the "less pure" fall back into the still for re-distillation.

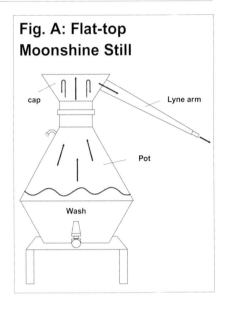

Fig. A: Flat-top Moonshine Still

cap

Lyne arm

Pot

Wash

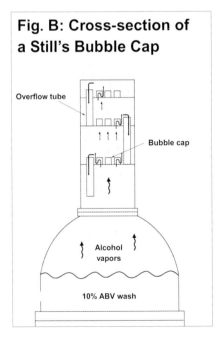

Fig. B: Cross-section of a Still's Bubble Cap

Overflow tube

Bubble cap

Alcohol vapors

10% ABV wash

Anatomy of a Craft Whiskey Still

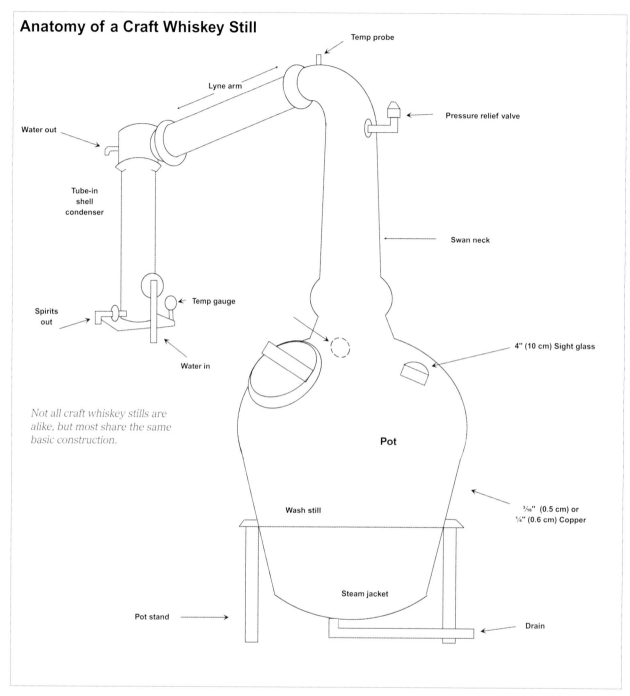

Temp probe

Lyne arm

Water out

Pressure relief valve

Tube-in shell condenser

Swan neck

Spirits out

Temp gauge

Water in

4" (10 cm) Sight glass

Not all craft whiskey stills are alike, but most share the same basic construction.

Pot

³⁄₁₆" (0.5 cm) or ¼" (0.6 cm) Copper

Wash still

Steam jacket

Pot stand

Drain

GOOSENECK STILL

The gooseneck pot still is the most common design of still used to produce Scottish malt whisky. Some Irish whiskies and a number of American and Canadian whiskies are also distilled in this type of still. This style of pot still has been in use for centuries for commercial whiskey production, and it is even more popular today in modern whiskey distilleries than ever.

The gooseneck still has a large round boiler and is functionally very similar to the crude pot still, except it has a long, broad neck rising from the boiler that allows enough separation to hold back most of the fusel alcohols from the distillate while retaining the desired flavors in the finished spirit. The neck bends at the top and connects to a pipe called a **lyne arm** that leads to a condenser coil immersed in water. The lyne arm

A gooseneck still clearly showing the lyne arm

usually angles downward slightly toward the condenser, but in some distilleries it tilts upward.

The level of separation in a gooseneck pot still is affected by the amount of condensation that takes place in the neck and lyne arm that falls back into the boiler. This condensation is called **reflux**, and the more reflux, the higher the level of separation. If the lyne arm is angled downward, then any vapor in the lyne arm that condenses will fall forward toward the condenser and become part of the distillate passing to the receiver. However, if the lyne arm is angled upward, condensation falls back to the boiler and will create additional reflux, and therefore additional separation.

Model of a gooseneck Forsyths whisky still

BEVERAGES PRODUCED IN GOOSENECK STILLS

Because the long, broad neck provides a large surface area, which results in a larger proportion of reflux than crude pot stills, gooseneck stills are more suitable for distilling beverage alcohol. The gooseneck stills are suited to the production of whiskey, brandy, rum, schnapps, and other non-neutral spirits, for which they are widely used commercially. However, they are not suitable for the production of vodka, gin, or other spirits derived from neutral alcohol, which requires a high-separation still capable of producing pure azeotrope ethanol.

The wash distilled in gooseneck stills is typically separated from the suspended solids, much like the malt washes used for making Scottish malt whisky. Some gooseneck stills are heated by an open fire under the boiler, which would result in the burning of suspended solids if they were in the wash. However, most contemporary stills are heated with steam jackets. This, combined with a **rummager**, can enable these stills to boil full mashes with all the grain in the boiler without burning the solids on the bottom of the pot.

A rummager is an agitating device that slowly turns around inside the still pot, dragging a net of copper chains along the bottom of the boiler to prevent solids from caking up and burning during distilling.

CONTINUOUS-RUN COLUMN STILL

This type of still is used for producing enormous volumes of spirit in a continuous operation that runs constantly for up to eleven months straight before it is shut down for cleaning and overhauling. They commonly have a fractionating column that stands about 100 feet (30.5m) high (similar to that of an oil refinery) and a series of bubble-cap trays spaced every couple of feet up the column. The trays are farther apart near the bottom and get closer together toward the top. It has no pot or boiler per se, and it is heated by blasting steam upward from the bottom of the column, while the wash is continuously fed into a tray at the middle of the column.

As the wash runs down through the trays of the column, it encounters the hot steam, which vaporizes the compounds in the wash and carries them up the column. The lower-boiling compounds continue to rise up the column while the higher-boiling ones condense and are carried down the column.

The column has an exit valve at every tray where vapor can be drawn off and led to a condenser. This enables the operators to configure the system so certain trays lead to a condenser that goes to the heads receiver, another set of trays can be sent to the hearts receiver, and other trays can be sent to the tails receiver. What flows to the bottom of the column is residue that is sent to the drain.

A possible configuration for bourbon would have the top two trays configured for heads, then the next four configured for hearts, the next five for tails, and the rest of the trays would reflux with no draw off and what reached the bottom would be discarded as residue.

The draw off rates would be set up to maintain a hearts phase with, say, a constant 65 percent ABV. Bourbon that's distilled in a continuous-run column still is usually done in two distillations, both with the hearts drawn off at about 65 percent ABV.

Because a continuous-run still runs for many months at a time, the wash must be fairly clear with a minimum of solids; otherwise, the buildup of residue in the system would become untenable and the system would need to be shut down to be cleaned. So, there is no process with a continuous-run still whereby the entire mash is distilled. The mash must always be strained or filtered before being placed in the reservoir supplying the still.

The distillery must have a battery of fermenters that are in constant operation at each stage of the fermentation process to keep up with the continuous demand for wash for the stills.

THE CONTINUOUS-RUN DESIGN FLAW

There is an inherent flaw in this design of still. Because the continuous-run still has a constant flow of new wash coming into it at all times, there are always heads and tails present in the column. This is unlike a batch still, which is any of the noncontinuous stills discussed in this text, where the heads are drawn off at the beginning of the run and then they are gone. In a continuous-run operation, all phases are constantly being introduced to the column by the incoming wash. This poses no problem with the tails, because at the trays where the hearts are drawn off, the tails are lower in the column and are therefore not present to be drawn off with the hearts. However, heads are still present at these trays, so no matter how well a continuous-run still is equilibrated there'll always be a small amount of heads in the hearts phase.

Having said this, the continuous-run column is a high-separation still that makes very precise separation of the compounds in its column. There is always going to be a trace amount of heads in the hearts, and this amount is still within the allowable limits for potable spirits. In most cases, it is less than the residual heads found in the hearts from commercial batch stills.

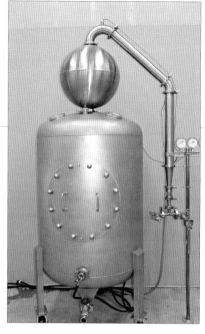

This alambic still was custom-built by Dynamic Alambic by reconfiguring a Grundig beer tank.

FRENCH CHARENTAIS ALAMBIC STILL

This type of still is used almost exclusively for making brandy, including cognac, Armagnac, Calvados, and other famous French brandies. It is designed especially to leave a lot of the aromatics and flavor in the distillate, and is therefore one of the lower-separation beverage-alcohol stills. Because of this quality, spirits are usually distilled twice in a French Charentais alambic still.

Whiskey can also be made in this design of still. It is functionally quite similar to the gooseneck still, but it creates a lower level of separation, making a richer and creamier-tasting whiskey, but with a little more fusel alcohol.

The French Charentais alambic still has three major components: the **boiler with helmet**, the **pre-heater**, and the **condenser**. The helmet is the chamber just above the boiler, and it serves as an expansion chamber, which works well to hold back a lot of the heavier compounds such as fusel alcohols and furfurols while allowing the desirable aromatics and flavors to be carried over in the distillate.

The pre-heater, as the name implies, preheats the next batch of wine to be distilled. It is also used as a reservoir to enable a near-continuous distillation process. Some brandy distillers simply include them as part of the hearts (not the heads). In this way, continuously feeding wine into the boiler is possible. Because there is no workable way to drain the boiler during operation, the continuous feeding of wine must stop when the boiler is too full to take any more.

Prior to a distillation run, the pre-heater is filled with wine to be heated for the next distillation. The pre-heater has the vapor tube from the boiler passing through it on its way to the condenser. This transfers heat from the vapor to the wine before the vapor enters the condenser. This heats the wine in the pre-heater to near boiling during the distillation run and reduces the amount of heat that the condenser has to dissipate, thereby making efficient use of heat and reducing the amount of cooling water used.

The pre-heater has a pipe with a valve leading from it to the

*Alambic still at **Jepson Vineyards** in Ukiah, California*

Alambic still installation in France

boiler. When a distillation run is finished and the boiler has been drained, the operator can open the valve and fill the boiler with another charge of wine from the pre-heater that's already at near-boiling temperature. This makes efficient use of heat and significantly reduces the amount of time to bring the next batch of wine to a boil.

The condenser in a French Charentais alambic still, as in most types of stills, consists of the copper coil immersed in a water jacket with cold water circulating around it.

BEVERAGES PRODUCED IN ALAMBIC STILLS

These stills are invariably used to distill wine, or in the case of whiskey, distiller's beer. They are not generally used to distill full mashes with all the solids left in. However, design-wise, the Charentais could be used to distill mashes with solids because its boiler is the same as that of the standard alambic, which is widely used to make grappa and marc from grape pomace. To do this, a sieve tray must be inserted into the boiler to serve as a false bottom to hold the solids above the bottom of the pot and prevent burning.

ARTISAN POT STILL

This type of still is the most versatile of all the stills. Each artisan pot still is nearly made to order, based on a distiller's needs and preferences. Its components include a spherical-shaped **boiler**, a **condenser**, and wide variety of optional components, such as a **steam jacket** or a **direct fire**, an **agitator**, a **helmet**, one or two **columns of bubble-cap trays**, a **dephlegmator**, and a **catalyzer**.

The spherical-shaped boiler evenly heats the substrate, particularly if there is an agitator. And, an artisan still that's steam heated and has an agitator can be used to distill any wash. Even washes full of fruit pulp or grain mash can be heated in this configuration of boiler without any risk of burning on the bottom of the pot. Also, by constantly agitating the wash throughout the distillation

run, the distillery can save about 20 percent on the heat required to perform the distillation.

The ability to distill the entire wash, including all the solids, purportedly gives a superior flavor to the spirit produced. Apparently, the fruit mashes for making schnapps yield a richer, more complex flavor if they can be distilled with all the fruit pulp in the boiler. Many whiskey distillers contend the same to be true for distilling grain mashes, and a number of the premium brands of American whiskey are distilled with the grain mash in the still.

The helmet component (optional) is technically an expansion chamber, and it is usually a nearly spherical dome that sits directly on top of the boiler. As vapor rises from the boiler, it passes through a comparatively narrow passageway into the larger volume of the helmet. This results in a sudden reduction in pressure, which helps hold back higher-boiling compounds while allowing desirable aromatics and flavors to continue up the column. Some distillers say this helmet is key to producing a truly excellent spirit.

From the helmet, the vapor rises into the column. In some artisan pot still configurations, the column is mounted directly on top of the helmet. When there is no helmet, the column is mounted directly on top of the boiler. In other configurations, such as two columns, the column is positioned beside the boiler. The reason for this is the still would stand too high for most facilities if the column were stacked on top of the helmet, or even on top of the boiler.

Within the column are bubble-cap trays. The vapor rises up the tubes under the bubble caps and bubbles out from under the cap and through the standing liquid on each tray. The standing liquid overflows at a certain depth to the next tray below. **Compound separation** takes place by the redistillation that occurs when the heat from the vapor transfers to the standing liquid. This causes higher-boiling compounds in the vapor to condense and lower-boiling compounds in the liquid to evaporate. The overall effect is to drive the lower-boiling compounds up the column in vapor state and the higher-boiling compounds down the column in liquid state.

Artisan pot still: the shape of the helmet "head" of the still influences the flavor of the distillate.

The Moor's cap on this alambic still has a distinctive look and gives a unique flavor profile to the distillates.

OPTIONAL STILL COMPONENTS

Modern artisan pot stills have an interesting feature that allows the operator to bypass any of the trays to vary the separation level for the column. There are levers on the side of the column connected to each tray, and the operator can position the lever to cause the tray to turn sideways and allow the vapors and liquid to pass by. Or the operator can position the lever the other way to put the tray in place so that it is fully engaged in processing reflux.

The dephlegmator resides above the top bubble-cap tray. It is a chamber at the top of the column with numerous vertical tubes for the vapor to travel through on its way to the condenser. There is a water jacket around the vertical tubes that the operator can flood with cooling water to increase the amount of reflux. The water level in the dephlegmator can be adjusted to give granular control over the amount of reflux.

Having the capability to dial up or down the reflux creates a great deal of control over the compound mix in the finished spirit. For example, if a given spirit had an excellent aroma and flavor profile but a rough finish due to an excess of fusel alcohol, the reflux could be dialed up slightly to hold back the fusel.

The catalyzer is positioned above the dephlegmator and has an array of sacrificial copper. Copper is an important material in a still because the noxious sulfides in the vapor instantly react out upon contact with copper. However, as this occurs over time, the copper material of the still becomes compromised, and expensive still components require replacing. The idea of the catalyzer is to have a chamber with copper in the vapor path specifically designed to react out the sulfides from the vapor. Over time, this copper erodes from the reaction with the sulfides, but it can be cheaply replaced. In effect, the copper in the catalyzer is being sacrificed to save the copper material of the still.

In summary, artisan pot stills can be superb stills and are well known for making quality spirits.

COLUMN CONFIGURATION

The number of bubble-cap trays in the column depends on the intended use of the artisan pot still, and it is therefore optional. Some artisan pot stills are used to make vodka and have two tall columns with a total of twenty bubble-cap trays. An excellent configuration for making whiskey, however, would be a still with a helmet, a column with four trays, a dephlegmator, and a catalyzer.

Unfortunately, their throughput is comparatively slow, and distilleries are often put in the position of having to opt for larger throughput stills, such as the continuous-run column, to meet the demands of their markets.

Artisan pot still

THE BATCH-STILL PROCESS OF DISTILLATION

THE DISTILLATION process is operationally the same for all four-batch stills discussed previously: the moonshine still, the gooseneck still, the French Charentais, and the artisan pot still. The continuous-run column still has a different regimen, and it is described in the section that follows.

HEADS, HEARTS, TAILS

In distilling parlance, the compounds in the wash that are not ethanol or water are called **congeners**. Some congeners, such as acetaldehyde, methanol, and certain esters and aldehydes, have lower boiling points than ethanol; certain other esters, the higher alcohols (fusel alcohols), and water have higher boiling points than ethanol. This means the lower-boiling congeners come out in high concentration at the beginning of a batch distillation run, and the higher-boiling ones come out in high concentration toward the end of the run, leaving the ethanol and the most desirable compounds as the most abundant components during the middle of the run.

When distillation takes place in a batch still, the distillate that comes out is divided into three phases called **heads**, **hearts**, and **tails**.

- *The heads contain the unwanted lower-boiling congeners that come out at the beginning of the run.*

- *The tails contain the unwanted higher-boiling congeners that come out at the end of the run.*

- *The hearts are the desired spirit in the middle.*

Because whiskey is not distilled at a high-separation level, it means that each phase bleeds into the adjacent phase. That is to say,

The Process of Distillation: An Overview

At left, the major steps from barley to barrel.
1. *Mash Tun: Used to convert barley grain starches to sugars*
2. *Fermentation of the wash*
3. *Stripping of the wash to remove water*
4. *Collection of "low wine" spirits*
5. *Redistilling the spirits to produce final spirits for barreling*
6. *Barreling or aging of spirits*

there is a considerable amount of ethanol in the heads phase, and there are late-heads congeners at the beginning of the hearts phase. Similarly, there is a significant amount of early-tails congeners at the end of the hearts, and there is a considerable amount of ethanol in the tails phase. The whiskey, comprised mostly of ethanol and water, has a delicate balance of late-heads and early-tails congeners that make up the flavor profile of the whiskey.

There are literally thousands of these congeners, or chemical flavor compounds, created during the distilling process, all of which have the potential of adding or subtracting to the desired final flavor profile of the distilled spirit. Part of the art (as opposed to the science) of distilling is knowing when these congeners are created, and when to add or remove them. In flavor-specific spirits, such as brandy and whiskey, it is desirable to carry over selected congeners into the finished spirit. However, in flavor-neutral spirits, such as vodka, the goal is to remove as many congeners as possible to end up with a spirit that has a clean, nonspecific palate.

Because both the heads and the tails contain a lot of ethanol and residual desirable flavor, they are mixed together and saved for future recovery. The heads and tails when mixed together are called **feints**. Feints can be distilled separately to produce another whiskey run, or they can be mixed in with a future spirit run, where their ethanol and flavors are recovered as a part of that run. However, each subsequent distillation produces its own set of heads, hearts, and tails, and the feints from those runs are also saved for future recovery.

TWO-RUN DISTILLATION

When whiskey is made, it is usually done in two distillation runs: a beer-stripping run and a spirit run.

- *The beer-stripping run is generally done in a larger, high-volume pot still called a* **beer stripper**. *The beer stripper is used to distill the fermented wash and concentrate the ethanol and all the impurities into a distillate of about 25 percent ethanol, called* **low wine**.

- *The spirit run is done in a smaller whiskey still, such as a gooseneck or an artisan reflux still, called a* **spirit still**. *The spirit still is used to distill the low wine and refine it into the finished spirit. There are the two outputs retained from the spirit run: the finished spirit and the feints.*

For a beer-stripping run, the fermented wash, which is typically about 8 percent ABV, is loaded into the beer stripper, and the contents are brought to a boil. Because this run is just a primary distillation, the heads, hearts, and tails are not separated out. The entire output from this run is collected in a single lot, and the run is continued until the aggregate percent alcohol is down to 25 percent ABV. This distillate is the low wine, which is the input to the spirit run.

To produce the finished whiskey, the spirit still is filled with the low wine from the beer-stripping run, and often a measure of feints from previous spirit runs. The spirit still is then brought to a boil.

It is with the spirit run that the distiller adjusts the boil-up rate to achieve a gentle, slow flow of distillate and carefully separates out the heads, hearts, and tails.

*Three pot stills at **Stoutridge Vineyard***

SINGLE-RUN DISTILLATION

Some whiskey distilleries produce their whiskey in a single distillation. They do a spirit run directly from the wash. The artisan reflux stills discussed previously are well suited to this type of whiskey distillation, but it is labor-intensive and the distiller must pay a lot of attention to numerous smaller runs rather than one larger run.

Some people find the whiskey from a single-distillation run to be richer and have a more natural flavor, while others find it to be harsh and unrefined. In the following text, the more common double-distillation method is used.

MAKING THE CUTS

Probably the most elusive part of the distilling process for making whiskey is making the cuts from heads to hearts and then to tails. **Making a cut** from one phase to the next is the point where the distiller switches the output so that it is collected in a different receiver than the previous phase. At the end of the spirit run, the heads will be in one container, the hearts in another, and the tails in a third one. The question is, when do you switch from one phase to the next?

Experienced distillers do this by taste. Even though there are measurable parameters such as still-head temperature and percent alcohol of the incoming spirit that can be used to judge when to make the cuts, taste and smell still remain the most reliable methods for determining them.

Here are the empirical parameters for judging the cuts.

- *The percent alcohol of the spirit that is flowing out of the still (i.e., the incoming spirit)*

- *The still-head temperature*

These vary from one still to the next, and they vary based on the properties of the low wine (e.g., percent alcohol and quantity). It is possible to develop a consistent process using the same still and the same quantity and formulation of low wine, such that the parameters remain the same for each run.

For example, in a spirit run in an artisan reflux still with low wine that is 25 percent ABV:

Begin-cut (i.e., the cut from heads to hearts) is usually done when the evolving distillate is at about 80 percent and when the still-head temperature is about 180°F (82°C).

End-cut (i.e., the cut from hearts to tails) is often done at about 65 percent and when the still-head temperature is about 201°F (94°C).

However, a spirit distilled from a straight malt wash can often be end-cut as low as 60 percent. Also, a gooseneck still distilling the very same wash may begin-cut at 72 percent and end-cut at 59 percent. Therefore, it is because of these nuances that smell and taste become the only truly reliable indicators of when to make the cuts.

BEGIN-CUT

When making the begin-cut, the taste characteristics that the distiller is looking for are as follows. When a spirit run comes to boil and the first distillate starts flowing from the still, this is the beginning of the heads phase. The distiller can collect a small sample of the distillate on a spoon or in a wineglass and smell it. At this stage, the distillate will have the sickening smell of solvents (such as nail-polish remover or paintbrush cleaner). However, before long this solvent smell diminishes, and even when a sample is tasted, these compounds will be very faint. As the solvent character disappears completely, the distillate will start to take on a hint of whiskey. This flavor will increase until it becomes very pronounced and highly concentrated. It is when this flavor is clearly evident but is still increasing in intensity that the distiller cuts to the hearts phase.

END-CUT

To make the end-cut, the distiller needs to monitor the flavor of

THE CONTINUOUS-RUN PROCESS OF DISTILLATION

the hearts through the following changes in taste. At the beginning of the hearts phase, the intensity of the whiskey flavor will still be increasing, and it will continue to do so until it becomes very strong. However, as the hearts continue, the intense whiskey flavor will fade into a smooth, sweet, pleasant flavor that will persist for most of the hearts. The flavor will change slightly as the hearts progress, but it will remain sweet and pleasant. Toward the end of the hearts, the flavor will start losing its sweetness, and a trace of harsh bitterness will begin to appear in the flavor. This harsh, bitter flavor is the onset of the tails. Although a small amount of this bitterness is considered to contribute to the "bite" character of the whiskey, the distiller should cut to the tails receiver before much of it is allowed to enter the hearts.

The tails can be collected until the evolving distillate is down to about 10 percent, and the still-head temperature is about 206°F or 208°F (97°C or 98°C). The reason for doing this is to render all the residual alcohol that is left in the still at the end of the hearts phase. This alcohol can then be recovered in a future spirit run.

The tails phase starts out bitter, and the bitterness becomes more intense as the tails continue, but as the tails progress, the bitterness subsides and gives way to a sweet-tasting water. This sweet water is called **backins**.

IN a continuous-run distillation process, wash is constantly entering the column, so all three phases (heads, hearts, and tails) are present in the column at all times. This means there can't be a discrete cut where the heads are drawn off and the hearts begin, or that the hearts end and the tails begin. All three phases must be drawn off at the same time.

A continuous-run column is a high-separation fractionating still that separates the compounds very well, so once the still is equilibrated and functioning in its steady state of operation, the distillers can determine which families of compounds are at each tray. For example, they might determine that the compounds coming out of the top two trays are heads compounds and route those

two trays to the heads receiver. Similarly, they might observe that the compounds coming out of the next four trays down are hearts. Then they might determine that the five trays below the hearts trays are producing tails and route them to the tails receiver. Below the tails trays just water would be coming out, and the valves would be closed, so it would be left to flow to the bottom of the column and then to a drain.

Because this type of still is not intermittent in its operation, it must be set up to constantly draw the three phases of distillate at all times. Although this is difficult to set up, it can produce very large quantities of spirit twenty-four hours a day for a long time.

Continuous run still

CHAPTER THREE

"Always carry a flagon of whiskey in case of snakebite, and furthermore, always carry a small snake."

— W.C. Fields, American actor and world-class drinker

WHISKEY

Stranahan's Colorado Whiskey

THIS chapter introduces the process of distilling a world's worth of whiskies, including North American styles of bourbon, Tennessee, rye, blended American, corn, and Canadian, and on to Scotch and Irish whiskies from Europe.

Of all of the basic categories of spirits, whiskey has spread the most across the world, achieving a geographic and stylistic diversity that is unmatched by any other type of distilled spirit. From the basic grain-based distilled spirits of ninth-century Ireland, Scotland, and northern Europe have evolved the classic whiskies of Scotland and Ireland. These spirits, in turn, served as the models for distillers in the newly settled North American colonies to produce what came to be first modern rye whiskey, and then in rapid succession, corn, bourbon, blended American, and Canadian whiskies.

All of these now classic styles of whiskey have, in recent decades, served as the stylistic inspiration for myriad new whiskies throughout the world, from Germany to Australia, and Nepal in between. Some of these new whiskies are based on existing styles. Japanese whisky distillers, for example, have generally taken their inspiration (and malt, and sometimes even their water) from Scotland. Others are boldly going forth in new directions, particularly among the new generation of American craft distillers.

THE HISTORY OF BOURBON WHISKEY

IN the early 1700s, a combination of bad economic times and religious unrest against the Anglican Church in Great Britain set off a wave of emigration from Scotland and Ireland. These Scots, Irish, and so-called "Scotch-Irish" (Protestants from the northern Irish county of Ulster) brought to North America their religion, their distrust of government control, and their skill at distilling whiskey.

This rush, augmented by German immigrants of a similar religious and cultural persuasion, passed through the seaboard colonies and settled initially in Pennsylvania, Maryland, and western Virginia. Mostly small farmers, they quickly adapted to growing rye because of its hardiness and, in the western counties, Native American corn because of its high yields. Grain was awkward to ship to East Coast markets because of the poor roads, so many farmers turned to distilling their crops

Whiskey barrels on display

into whiskey. In Pennsylvania, these were primarily rye whiskies; farther to the west and south corn whiskies predominated. By

the end of the American War of Independence in 1784, the first commercial distilleries had been established in what was then the western Virginia county of Kentucky. From the start, they produced corn-based whiskies.

In 1794, the cash-strapped federal government imposed the first federal excise tax on distillers. The farmer-distillers of western Pennsylvania responded violently. Federal tax agents were assaulted and killed by angry mobs. Order was finally restored when the federal government sent in an army of 15,000 militiamen, led by George Washington, to put down the revolt. The ringleaders were convicted and sentenced to be hanged. But cooler heads prevailed, and after jail time they

NOT-SO-TRIVIAL PURSUIT

The first waves of British settlers in North America were a thirsty lot. It is recorded that the Pilgrims chose to make final landfall in Massachusetts, even though their original destination was Virginia, primarily because they were almost out of beer.

The first locally made alcoholic beverage was beer, although the limited supply of barley malt was frequently supplemented by everything from spruce tips to pumpkin. Distilled spirits soon followed, with rum made from imported Caribbean molasses dominating in the northern colonies and an assortment of fruit brandies in the South.

Label for **Hudson Baby Bourbon** by **Tuthilltown Spirits**

were pardoned and released.

This situation did provoke a new migration of settlers through the Cumberland Gap and into the then-western frontier lands of Kentucky and Tennessee. In these new states, farmers found ideal corn-growing country and smooth limestone-filtered water, two of the basic ingredients of bourbon whiskey.

The name *bourbon* comes from a county in eastern Kentucky, which in turn was named for the Bourbon kings of France, who had aided the American rebels in the Revolu-

tionary War. Bourbon County was in the early nineteenth century a center of whiskey production and transshipping. (Ironically, at the present time, it is a "dry" county.) The local whiskey, made primarily from corn, soon gained a reputation for being particularly smooth because the local distillers aged their products in charred oak casks. The adoption of the "sour mash" grain conversion technique further distinguished bourbon from other whiskey styles.

By the 1840s, bourbon was recognized and marketed

Benjamin Prichard's Double Barreled Bourbon from **Prichards' Distillery**

Label for **Pappy Van Winkle's Family Reserve Kentucky Straight Bourbon Whiskey**

as a distinctive American style of whiskey, although not as a regionally specific spirit. Bourbon came to be produced in Kentucky, Tennessee, Indiana, Illinois, Ohio, Missouri, Pennsylvania, North Carolina, and Georgia, although the only legal requirement for calling a whiskey "bourbon" is that it be produced in the United States. Nowadays, bourbon production is slowly expanding to other states as new craft whiskey distillers come online. Initially bourbon was made in pot stills, but as the century progressed the new column still technology was increasingly adopted. The last old-line pot still plant closed in Pennsylvania in 1992, but the technique was revived in Kentucky in 1995 when the historic Labrot & Graham Distillery was renovated and reopened with a set of new, Scottish-built copper pot stills. More recently, most of the new generation of craft whiskey distillers use pot stills.

The late nineteenth century saw the rise of the temperance movement, a social phenomenon driven by a potent combination of religious and women's groups. Temperance societies, such as the Women's Christian Temper-

REVIVAL OF THE FITTEST

It may seem odd, but Scotch whisky may be bourbon's inspiration for long-term revival. The steady growth in sales of single malt and high-quality Scotch whiskies has not gone unnoticed in bourbon country. All of the Kentucky and Tennessee whiskey distilleries are now marketing high-end "single cask" and "small batch" whiskies that have found great success among upscale consumers. More than thirty craft whiskey distilleries have opened in the past few years across the United States to cater to this increasing demand for quality over quantity. The United States may yet, in the words of one commentator, "turn away from foreign potions and return to its native spirit."

Label for **Blanton's Single Barrel Kentucky Straight Bourbon Whiskey** *by* **Buffalo Trace Distillery**

ance Union and the Anti-Saloon League, operated nationally, but they were particularly active in the Southern states. The notion of temperance soon gave way to a stated desire for outright prohibition, and throughout the rest of the century an assortment of states and counties adopted prohibition for varying lengths of time and degrees of severity. This muddle of legal restrictions played havoc in the bourbon industry, because it interfered with the production and aging of stocks of whiskey.

National Prohibition in 1919 had effects on the bourbon industry beyond shutting down most of the distilleries. Drinking did not stop, of course, and the United States was soon awash in illegal alcohol, much of it of dubious

Souvenir bottle of Evan Williams Kentucky Straight Bourbon Whiskey by **Heaven Hill Distilleries**

quality. What did change was the American taste in whiskey. Illicit moonshine and imported Canadian whiskeys were lighter in taste and body than bourbon and rye. The corresponding increase in popularity of white spirits such as gin and vodka further altered the marketplace. When Repeal came in 1933, a number of the old distilleries didn't reopen, and the industry began a slow consolidation that lasted into the early 1990s, at which time there were only ten distilleries in Kentucky and two in Tennessee.

Bottle of **Four Roses Distillery's Single Barrel Kentucky Straight Bourbon Whiskey**

Middle:
Elijah Craig 18-year-old Kentucky Straight Bourbon Whiskey *by* **Heaven Hill Distilleries**

Right:
Buffalo Trace Distillery's Kentucky Straight Bourbon Whiskey

TENNESSEE WHISKEY

Tennessee whiskey is a first cousin of bourbon, with virtually an identical history. The same sort of people used the same sort of grains and the same sort of production techniques to produce a style of whiskey that, remarkably, is noticeably different. The early whiskey distillers in Tennessee, for reasons that are lost to history, added a final step to their production process when they began filtering their whiskey through thick beds of sugar-maple char-coal. This filtration removes some of the congeners (flavor elements) in the spirit and creates a smooth, mellow palate. The two remaining whiskey distillers in the state continue this tradition, which a distiller at the Jack Daniel's Distillery once described as being "same church, different pew."

RYE WHISKEY

The Scotch-Irish immigrant distillers had some exposure to using rye in whiskey production, but for their German immigrant neighbors, rye had been the primary grain used in the production of schnapps and vodka back in northern Europe. They continued this distilling practice, particularly in Pennsylvania and Maryland, where rye whiskey, with its distinctive hard-edged, grainy palate, remained the dominant whiskey type well into the twentieth century.

Rye whiskey was more adversely affected by National Prohibition than bourbon was. A generation of consumers weaned on light-bodied and relatively delicate white spirits turned away from the pungent, full-bodied straight rye whiskies. Production of rye whiskies had vanished altogether from the Mid-Atlantic states by the 1980s. A handful of modern rye whiskies are currently being made by bourbon distilleries in Kentucky and Indiana. The United States's first indigenous whiskey style is today only barely surviving in the marketplace. Its primary use is for blending to give other

Hudson Manhattan Rye Whiskey by Tuthilltown Spirits

*Below: The hand-blown bottle of **Rendezvous Rye Whiskey** casts a wavy amber shadow on a gift box*

Label for
Rye Whiskey
from the
**Isaiah Morgan
Distillery**

*A bottle of **Mellow Corn,
Kentucky Straight Corn
Whiskey** by **Medley Company***

whiskies more character and backbone, although a small but vocal group of rye whisky enthusiasts continue to champion it, and a number of new craft distillers are again producing their interpretations of this classic American whiskey style.

BLENDED AMERICAN WHISKEY

Blended whiskies date from the early nineteenth century when the invention of the column still made possible the production of neutral spirits. Distillers blended one or more straight whiskies (bourbon and rye) with these neutral spirits in varying proportions to create their own branded blend. The taste and quality of these whiskies, then as now, varies according to the ratio of straight whiskey to neutral grain spirit. Early blends were frequently flavored with everything from sherry to plug tobacco. Compared to straight whiskies, they were inexpensive and bland. Modern blends utilize dozens of different straight whiskies to ensure a consistent flavor profile. Blended American whiskies had a great sales boost during and just after World War II, when distillers promoted them as a way of stretching their limited supply of straight whiskey. Blended whiskeys were considered to be too bland by bourbon and rye drinkers, and consumers with a taste for lighter spirits soon migrated over to vodka and gin.

CORN WHISKEY

Corn whiskey, an unaged, clear spirit, was the first truly American whiskey, and the precursor to bourbon. Scotch-Irish farmers produced it in their stills for family consumption or to trade for store goods. When state and federal excise taxes were permanently

*Old Potrero 18th Century Style Rye Whiskey by **Anchor Distilling***

*A bottle of **Platte Valley Straight Corn Whiskey** by McCormick Distilling Co.*

CANADIAN WHISKY

Canadian whiskies, as with their American cousins, originated on the farm. These early whiskies were made primarily from rye, though over time Canadian distillers turned to corn, wheat, and other grains. Canadians continue to refer to their whisky as "rye," even though the mash bill is now predominantly a mix of corn, wheat, and barley. Several of the new generation of Canadian craft distillers are, however, marketing both all-malt and "true" rye whiskies.

introduced during the Civil War, most of the production of corn whiskey went underground to become moonshine, where it has remained ever since. A modest amount of commercial corn whiskey is still produced and consumed in the South, while an increasing number of craft whiskey distilleries are now experimenting with this more interesting alternative to vodka.

Above:
*A bottle of **Snake River Stampede Blended Canadian Whisky***

Left:
Forty Creek Small Batch Reserve Whisky** (Canadian) by **Kittling Ridge Estate Wines & Spirits

THE BASIS OF NORTH AMERICAN WHISKIES

Whiskey barrels on display on an antique truck

A cooper shoots air into a charring barrel to stoke the flames.

A cooper forms a barrel before attaching hoops around the outside.

NORTH American whiskies are all-grain spirits that have been produced from a mash bill that usually mixes together corn, rye, wheat, barley, and other grains in different proportions, and then is aged for an extended period of time in wooden barrels. These barrels may be new or used, and charred or uncharred on the inside, depending on the type of whiskey being made.

Most non-craft North American whiskies are made in column stills. The United States government requires that all whiskies:

- Be made from a grain mash.

- Be distilled at 90 percent ABV or less.

- Be reduced to no more than 62.5 percent ABV (125° proof) before being aged in oak barrels (except for corn whiskey, which does not have to be aged in wood).

- Have the aroma, taste, and characteristics that are generally attributed to whiskey.

- Be bottled at no less that 40 percent ABV (80° proof).

CLASSIFICATIONS OF NORTH AMERICAN WHISKIES

NORTH AMERICAN whiskies are essentially classified by the type or variety of grains in the mash bill, the percentage or proof of alcohol at which they are distilled, and the duration and manner of their aging.

A stirring paddle sits over a moonshine wash.

STYLE	DEFINITION	HOWEVER...
Bourbon Whiskey	Must contain a minimum of 51 percent corn, be produced in the United States, be distilled at less than 80 percent ABV (160° proof), and be aged for a minimum of two years in new charred barrels	In practice, virtually all straight whiskies are aged for at least four years. Any bourbon—or any other domestic or imported whiskey—that is aged less than four years must contain an age statement on the label.
Small Batch Bourbon	Bourbons that are bottled from a small group of specially selected barrels that are blended together	The choice of barrels is purely subjective on the part of the master blender.
Single Barrel Bourbon	Bourbon from one specific cask	The choice of the barrel is purely subjective on the part of the master blender.
Tennessee Whiskey	Must contain a minimum of 51 percent corn, be distilled at less than 80 percent ABV (160° proof), be filtered through a bed of sugar-maple charcoal, and be aged for a minimum of two years in new charred barrels	In recent years, as the sales volume of Tennessee whiskies has increased, the aging on many of the major brands beyond the required minimum of two years has decreased. You have been warned.
Rye Whiskey	Must contain a minimum of 51 percent rye grain, be distilled at less than 80 percent ABV (160° proof), and be aged for a minimum of two years in new charred barrels	Rye whiskey's dry, peppery, astringent character requires at least four years of aging to soften its otherwise hard edge.
Blended American Whiskey	Must contain at least 20 percent straight whiskey, with the balance being unaged neutral spirit or, in a few cases, high-proof light whiskey	It has a general whiskey flavor profile (most closely resembling bourbon), but lacks any defining taste characteristic.

Barley growing in a field in Washington State

STYLE	DEFINITION	HOWEVER...
Corn Whiskey	This commercial product must contain at least 80 percent corn, be distilled at less than 80 percent ABV (160° proof), and be aged for a minimum of two years in new or used uncharred barrels.	Corn whiskey is the exception to the rule that requires whiskey to be aged to reach its full flavor potential. Well-made corn whiskey has a bright, fruity, almost sweet palate that fades with time.
Moonshine Whiskey (aka white lightning, corn likker, white dog)	Distilled from a mix of corn and sugar and aged in Mason jars and jugs	It is aged for the length of time that it takes the customers to get home or the Dukes of Hazzard to make a delivery in the General Lee.
Canadian Whisky	Made primarily from corn or wheat, with a supplement of rye, barley, or barley malt. There are no Canadian government requirements for the percentages of grains used in the mash bill. They are aged, primarily in used oak barrels, for a minimum of three years, with most brands being aged for four to six years.	Virtually all Canadian whiskies (except the pot-distilled malt whiskies of Glenora in Nova Scotia) are blended from different grain whiskies of different ages.
Bulk Canadian Whiskies	Usually shipped in barrels to their destination country, where they are bottled. These bulk whiskies are usually bottled at 40 percent ABV (80° proof) and are usually no more than four years old.	Additional aging statements on the labels of some of these whiskies should be treated with deep skepticism.
Bottled in Canada Whiskies	Generally have older whiskies in their blends and are bottled at 43.4 percent ABV (86.8° proof)	Age, in this context, is still a relative thing. Ten-year-old Canadian whisky is considered a really, really old whisky.

Peregrine Rock Single Malt Whiskey by St. James Spirits

NORTH AMERICAN WHISKEY REGIONS

North America's variations of whiskey are as nuanced and distinct as the continent's regions. Most are aged in new wood barrels, but beyond that there has been much experimenting in recent years.

UNITED STATES

Kentucky produces all types of North American whiskies except for Tennessee and Canadian. It currently has the largest concentration of whiskey distilleries on the continent, but may soon cede that claim to Michigan, Colorado, or one of the Pacific Northwest states as new craft distilleries continue to open.

*Barrels of bourbon aging at the **Woodford Reserve Distillery***

Most Wanted Kansas Whiskey by **High Plains Inc.**

Tennessee started out as bourbon country, but today its two remaining whiskey distilleries specialize in the distinctive Tennessee style of whiskey.

Other states—primarily Indiana, Illinois, Virginia, and Missouri—have large distilleries that produce straight whiskeys, although some of these plants are currently mothballed.

CANADA

Ontario has the largest concentration of whisky distilleries in Canada, with three. Alberta has two, and Manitoba, Quebec, and Nova Scotia each have one. With the exception of Glenora in Nova Scotia and Kittling Ridge in Ontario, all of the other current Canadian whisky distilleries produce only blended Canadian whisky, although a number of new craft whisky distilleries are listed in the index.

REGIONAL FLAVORS

There are now more than thirty craft distilleries in at least seventeen states that are producing such standard whiskey styles as bourbon, corn, and rye, as well as many experimental variations. One example is Wasmund's Single Malt Whiskey from the Copper Fox Distillery of Sperryville, Virginia. This distillery has its own floor maltings and soaks its aging spirit in applewood chips. This sort of production twist, which has its roots in craft brewing, is increasingly becoming a distinctive feature of American craft distilling.

Additionally, there are a number of distilling plants scattered around the country that rectify (redistill), process, and bottle spirits that were originally distilled elsewhere. These distilleries, in addition to sometimes bottling bourbon that has been shipped to them in bulk, may also create their own blended whiskies. These whiskies tend to be relatively inexpensive "well" brands that are sold mainly to taverns and bars for making mixed drinks.

Rick Wasmund malts barley by hand at the **Copper Fox Distillery**.

A Whiskey Lexicon

Bonded whiskey is bourbon from a single distillery that was produced in a single "season" and then aged for at least four years in a government-supervised "bonded" warehouse. Distillers originally did this to avoid having to pay the excise tax until the whiskey was aged and ready for market. Consumers came to (erroneously) regard the "bottled in bond" designation as a statement of quality. Bonded whiskies are not much of a factor in today's market, although they still exist.

The mash is the mix of crushed grain (including some malt that contains enzymes to break down grain starches into sugars) and hot water from which the distiller draws a liquid extract called wort. The wort is fermented into a simple beer called the wash, which is then distilled.

Sour mash is the fermentation process by which a percentage of a previous fermentation is added to a new batch as a "starter" to get the fermentation going and maintain a level of consistency from batch to batch. A sweet mash means that only fresh yeast is added to a new batch to start fermentation.

Straight whiskey is unblended whiskey that contains no neutral spirit. Bourbon, Tennessee, rye, and corn whiskies are straight whiskies. There is also a spirit, simply called "straight whiskey," that is made from a mixture of grains, none of which accounts for 51 percent of the mash bill.

In this whiskey barrel storage building, a black mold and rust thrive on the "angel's share" of evaporated alcohol and the Kentucky humidity.

Wash being made in the mash tun

Bubbles rise during a grain fermentation.

Scotch Whisky, Irish Whiskey, and Other Whiskies of the World

WHISKY is defined, in its most basic sense, as a spirit that is distilled from grain. Sometimes the grain has been malted, sometimes not. What distinguishes whisky from vodka, gin, aquavit, and other grain-based spirits is that it is aged, often for long periods of time, in wooden barrels (usually oak). This barrel aging smoothes the rough palate of the raw spirit, adding aromatic and flavoring nuances along with the base amber hue that sets whiskies apart from white grain spirits.

The History of Scotch Whisky

The basis of Scotch whisky is the heather-flavored ales made from barley malt that the Picts and their prehistoric ancestors brewed. Archeologists have found evidence of such brewing dating back to at least 2000 BCE. This ale, still produced today by at least one Scottish microbrewer, was low in alcohol and not very stable.

Starting in the ninth century, Irish monks arrived in Scotland to Christianize their Celtic brethren. They brought along the first primitive stills, which they had picked up during their proselytizing visits to mainland Europe during the Dark Ages. The local Picts soon found that they could create a stable alcoholic beverage by distilling heather ale. Simple stills came to be found in most rural homesteads, and homemade whisky became an integral part of Gaelic culture.

Forsyth stills at the **Penderyn Whisky Distillery** *in Wales*

*Laphroaig 10-year-old
Single Malt Scotch Whisky
from the Island of Islay*

*Talisker 18-year-old Single
Malt Scotch Whisky*

WHY BLENDED SCOTCH WHISKY IS A GOOD THING, EVEN IF YOU PREFER SINGLE MALTS

It is a truism of religion that converts frequently become the most zealous of believers. Among freshly minted modern-day enthusiasts of Scotch malt whiskies, it is a frequently heard refrain that malt whiskies are superior to the blended article, and that the latter are just not worth bothering with. Personal taste is ultimately subjective, of course. But single malt drinkers should raise their hats in salute whenever a Dewar's or Johnnie Walker delivery truck drives by, because without these blended brands most of the remaining malt distilleries would not exist. Blended Scotch whiskies require a blend of dozens of different malt whiskies to be combined with the grain whisky to create the desired blend. The individual percentages of each malt whisky may be small, but each contributes its unique character to the blend. A blender will thus need to buy or produce a large amount of different malt whiskies to maintain the consistency of the blend. Thus, for a malt whisky distillery, the single malt may get all of the glory, but the blends ultimate pay the bills.

*Highland Park 12-year-old
Single Malt Scotch Whisky*

As long as Scottish kings ruled the country from Edinburgh the status quo of whisky as just another farm product was more or less maintained. But the Act of Union in 1707 that combined England, Wales, and Scotland into the United Kingdom altered the Scotch whisky scene forever. The London government soon levied excise taxes on Scottish-made whisky (while at the same time cutting the taxes on English gin). The result was a predictable boom in illicit distilling. In 1790s Edinburgh it was estimated that more thn 400 illegal stills competed with just eight licensed distilleries. A number of present-day Scottish distilleries, particularly in the Highlands, have their origins in such illicit operations.

The Excise Act of 1823 reduced taxes on Scotch whisky tolerably. This act coincided with the dawn of the industrial revolution, and entrepreneurs were soon building new, state-of-the-art distilleries. The local moonshiners (called smugglers) did not go quietly. Some of the first licensed distillers in rural locations were threatened by their illicit peers. But in the end, production efficiencies and the rule of law won out. The whisky that came from these distilleries was made exclusively from malted barley that had been kiln dried over peat fires. The smoke from these peat fires gave the malt a distinctive tang that made the Scottish product instantly identifiable by whisky drinkers all over the world.

The nineteenth century brought a rush of changes to the Scotch whisky industry. The introduction of column stills early in the 1830s led to the creation of grain whisky, which in turn led to blended Scotch whisky in the late 1860s. The smooth blandness of the grain whisky toned down the assertive smoky character of the malt whiskies.

The resulting blended whisky was milder and more acceptable to foreign consumers, particularly the English, who turned to Scotch whisky in the 1870s when a phylloxera infestation (an insect pest that destroys grape vines) in

*Barrels aging at the **Penderyn Whisky Distillery** in Wales*

*Keith Tench, visitor centre manager, poses with distiller **Gillian Howell** at the **Penderyn Whisky Distillery** in Wales.*

the vineyards of Europe disrupted supplies of cognac and port, two of the mainstays of civilized living. Malt whisky distilleries were bought up by blending companies, and their output was blended with grain whiskies to create the great blended brands that have come to dominate the market. The malt whisky distilleries took a backseat to these brands and sold most or, in some cases, all of their production to the blenders. The recent popular revival of malt whiskies has led most of the distilleries to come out with bottlings of their own products.

By the 1970s, international liquor companies owned most of the malt whisky distilleries, a situation that continues to this day.

THE HISTORY OF IRISH WHISKEY

The Scots most likely learned about distilling from the Irish (though they are loath to admit it). The Irish in turn learned about it, according to the Irish at least, from missionary monks who arrived in Ireland in the seventh century. The actual details are a bit sketchy for the next 700 years or so, but it does seem that monks in various monasteries were distilling *aqua vitae* ("water of life"), primarily for making medical compounds. These first distillates were probably grape or fruit brandy rather than grain spirit. Barley-based whiskey (the word derives from *uisce beatha*, the Gaelic interpretation of aqua vitae) first appears in the historical

record in the mid-1500s, when the Tudor kings began to consolidate English control in Ireland. Queen Elizabeth I was said to be fond of it and had casks shipped to London regularly.

The imposition of an excise tax in 1661 had the same effect as it did in Scotland, with the immediate commencement of the production of *poteen* (the Irish version of moonshine). This did not, however, slow the growth of the distilling industry, and by the end of the eighteenth century there were more than 2,000 stills in operation.

Under British rule, Ireland was export oriented, and Irish distillers produced large quantities of pot-distilled whiskey for export into the expanding British Empire (along with grains and assorted

A group tour marvels at the gleaming column stills at a craft distillery.

DISTILLING TIMELINE

SPIRIT TYPE	FERMENTATION	MIN. AGING	MAX. AGING
BRANDIES			
Brandy V.S.	3 weeks	2 years	5 years
Brandy VSOP	3 weeks	4 years	15 years
Brandy X.O.	3 weeks	6 years	20–30 years
Grappa	1 week	1 month	3 years
Apple Brandy	3 weeks	2 years	20 years
Fruit Brandy	3 weeks	4–6 months	4 years
WHISKIES			
Scotch	1 week	3 years	30 years
Irish	1 week	3 years	10 years
Bourbon	1 week	2 years	20 years
Tennessee	1 week	2 years	6 years
Rye	1 week	2 years	25 years
Corn	4 days	2 years	2 years
Canadian	1 week	3 years	10 years
Moonshine	4 days	1 week	1 week
RUMS			
White	3 days	2 months	2 years
Golden	3 days	1 year	3 years
Dark	1 week	1 year	4 years
Añejo/Aged	1 week	5 years	30 years
TEQUILAS			
Blanco	1 week	None	2 months
Reposado	1 week	3 months	9 months
Añejo/Aged	1 week	1 year	4 years
VODKAS			
All	3 days	None	3 months
GINS			
Dry	3 days	None	None
Genever	1 week	1 year	3 years

foodstuffs). In the late nineteenth century, more than 400 brands of Irish whiskey were being exported and sold in the United States.

This happy state of affairs lasted into the early twentieth century, when the market began to change. The Irish pot still users were slow to respond to the rise of blended Scotch whisky with its column-distilled, smooth-grain-whisky component. When National Prohibition in the United States closed off their largest export market, many of the smaller distilleries closed. The remaining distilleries then failed to anticipate the coming of Repeal (unlike the Scotch distillers) and were caught short when it came. The Great Depression, trade embargoes between the newly independent Irish Republic and the United Kingdom, and World War II caused further havoc among the distillers.

In 1966, the three remaining distilling companies in the Republic of Ireland—Powers, Jameson, and Cork Distilleries—merged into a single company, Irish Distillers Company (IDC). In

Yamazaki Distillery
Shimamoto, Osaka,
Japan
12-year-old
Single Malt Whisky
(Japan)

Karuizawa Number
One Single Cask
Whisky (Japan). The
distillery is located in the
foothills of Mount Asama,
and active volcano.

in 1989, when a potato-peel ethanol plant in Dundalk was converted into a whiskey distillery. The new Cooley Distillery began to produce malt and grain whiskeys, with the first three-year-old bottlings released in 1992.

THE HISTORY OF JAPANESE WHISKY

The modern Japanese whisky industry can trace its beginnings back to one man, Masataka Taketsura. The son of a sake brewer, Taketsura went to Scotland in 1918 and spent two years studying chemistry at Glasgow University and working at a Scotch whisky distillery in Rothes in the Highlands. He returned to Japan in 1920 with a Scottish bride and a determination to change the Japanese distilling industry.

The Japanese were then, as they are now, major consumers of Scotch whisky. Locally produced spirits, however, were limited to the fiery sorghum- or sweet-potato-based shochu, and a handful of dubious "whiskies" that were little more than neutral spirits colored with caramel. Taketsura convinced the owners of what became the Suntory Company to begin production of barley malt and grain whiskies based on the Scottish model. These whiskies, some of which are made from imported peat-smoked Scottish malt, became very successful in the Japanese market. Other distilleries followed Suntory's lead, and these whiskies, based on Scotch whisky models (and later bourbon whis-

1972, Bushmills, the last distillery in Northern Ireland, joined IDC. In 1975, IDC opened a new mammoth distillery at Midleton near Cork, and all of the other distilleries in the republic were closed down with the production of their brands being transferred to Midleton. For a fourteen-year period, the Midleton plant and Bushmills in Northern Ireland were the only distilleries in Ireland.

This sad state of affairs ended

key), soon dominated the market.

Modern Japanese distillers (including the Nikka Whisky Distillery, which was founded by Taketsura in 1934) have followed this trend and nowadays produce and market a full range of malt and blended whiskies.

STYLE	DEFINITION	HOWEVER...
Single Malt Scotch Whisky	Malt whisky that has been produced at one distillery. It may be a mix of malt whiskies from different years. The barley malt for Scotch whisky is first dried over fires that have been stoked with dried peat. The peat smoke adds a distinctive smoky tang.	If it contains a mix of whiskies from different years, the age statement on the bottle label gives the age of the youngest spirit in the mix.
Vatted Malt Scotch Whisky	Blend of malt whiskies from different Scottish distilleries	A much underrated style, for no good reason. The term blended malt whisky means the same thing.
Scotch Grain Whisky	Made from wheat or corn with a small percentage of barley and barley malt	Rarely bottled, but well-aged examples can be delicate drams.
Blended Scotch Whisky	Blend of grain whiskey and malt whiskey	The ratio of malt whisky to grain whisky in the blend can vary considerably among brands. And the number of malt whiskies in the malt whisky component can range from a handful to dozens.
Irish Pot Still Whiskey	Unless labeled as such, Irish whiskeys are a mix of pot- and column-distilled whiskeys.	Once upon a time, all Irish whiskies were pot distilled. Column stills were for Scots.
Irish Malt Whiskey	Can be pot distilled, column distilled, or a mixture of both	Irish malts have made a welcome comeback in recent years.
Irish Whiskey	A blend of malt and grain whiskies	The ratio of malt to grain whiskey can vary widely, which is not necessarily reflected in the price.
Japanese Malt Whisky	Produced in pot stills from lightly peated barley malt	Broadly modeled on Scottish Highland Malt Whiskies, and in some cases done very well indeed.
Japanese Whisky	A blend of malt whisky (Japanese or Scotch) and domestically produced grain whisky	Not to be confused with Shochu, native Japanese whisky, which is made from rice, sorghum, or barley, and is a very different earthy sort of spirit.
New Zealand Single Malt Whisky	Pot-distilled malt whisky	New Zealand whisky distilleries open and close with the frequency of rugby sports bars, so good luck finding any.
New Zealand Blended Whisky	A mix of domestic malt and grain whiskies	Occasionally it may even have some domestically made whisky in it.
Australian Whisky	All currently produced Australian whiskies are pot-distilled malt whiskies	Tasmania is the center of the new generation of Australian whisky distilling.

Thousands of barrels stacked outside a cooperage

THE HISTORY OF NEW ZEALAND AND AUSTRALIAN WHISKY

Scottish emigrants brought their whisky-making skills to New Zealand in the 1840s. A thriving whisky industry soon developed and operated until 1875, when new, excessively high excise taxes and heavy competition from imported British whiskies forced the local commercial distilleries to shut down. A new, almost commercial-sized moonshine trade quickly replaced them, a situation that continued for almost a century.

In 1968 a new whisky distillery opened in Dunedin. It produces a range of malt and grain whiskies, broadly in the Scottish style, from locally grown grain. Even the barley malt is kilned and smoked using local peat.

Australian whisky production has experienced a similar varied history, with assorted nineteenth-century producers popping up in the various states, only to be driven out of business by British imports. Abortive attempts in the 1990s to revive whisky production have been followed more recently by a new generation of more successful craft whisky distillers, particularly on the island of Tasmania.

THE BASIS OF SCOTCH WHISKY, IRISH WHISKEY, JAPANESE WHISKY, AND NEW ZEALAND AND AUSTRALIAN WHISKY

All of these whiskey styles, while very different in taste and style, are based on malted barley as the dominant source of flavor and character.

SCOTLAND

There are two basic categories of Scotch whisky: malt whisky, which is made exclusively from malted barley that has been dried over smoking peat fires, and grain whisky, which is made from unmalted wheat or corn. These whiskies are aged in used wooden bourbon or sherry barrels for a minimum of three years, although five to ten years is the general practice.

IRELAND

There are two basic categories of Irish whiskey: malt whiskey, which is made exclusively from malted barley that has been kiln-dried, but *not* over peat fires, and grain whiskey, which is made from unmalted wheat or corn. These whiskeys are aged in used wooden bourbon or sherry barrels for a minimum of three years, although five to eight years is the norm.

JAPAN

Japanese whiskies, both malt and blended, are broadly based on Scotch whiskies, with some top brands even being made with imported Scottish water and peat-smoked barley malt. The peat-smoke character of Japanese whiskies is generally more subtle and delicate than their Scottish counterparts. Japanese whiskies may be aged in both new and used (usually bourbon) wooden barrels, which may be either charred or uncharred.

NEW ZEALAND AND AUSTRALIA

New Zealand and Australian whiskies both draw on Scottish, Irish, and American traditions in a cheerfully mixed manner, using both peated and unpeated locally-grown barley malt to produce mostly pot-distilled malt whiskies that are aged in used bourbon and wine barrels for a theoretical, if not always absolute, minimum of six years for malt whisky.

Detail of fermenting barley wash for making whiskey

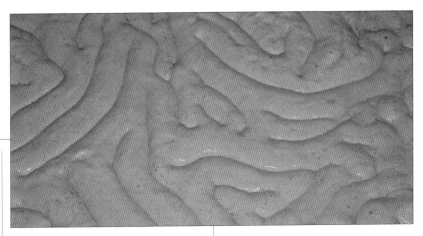

THE DISTILLATION OF SCOTCH WHISKY, IRISH WHISKEY, JAPANESE WHISKY, AND NEW ZEALAND AND AUSTRALIAN WHISKY

Double- and even triple-distillation is the norm for this family of barley malt–based whiskies.

SCOTLAND

All Scotch malt whiskies are double distilled in pot stills, whereas Scotch grain whiskies are made in column stills.

IRELAND

Irish whiskeys, both blended and malt, are usually triple distilled through both column and pot stills, although there are a few exclusively pot-distilled brands.

JAPAN

Japanese whiskies follow the Scottish tradition, with malt whiskies being double distilled in pot stills and grain whiskies in column stills.

NEW ZEALAND AND AUSTRALIA

Both New Zealand and Australian malt and grain whiskies are double distilled in pot stills, with some Tasmanian distilleries reportedly experimenting with triple distillation.

SCOTCH WHISKY, IRISH WHISKEY, JAPANESE WHISKY, AND NEW ZEALAND AND AUSTRALIAN WHISKY REGIONS

SCOTLAND

The Highlands consist of the portion of Scotland north of a line from Dundee on the North Sea coast in the east to Greenock on the Irish Sea in the west, including all of the islands off the mainland except for Islay. Highland malt whiskies cover a broad spectrum of styles. They are generally considered aromatic, smooth, and medium bodied, with palates that range from lush complexity to floral delicacy. The subregions of the Highlands include Speyside; the North, East, and West Highlands; the Orkney Isles; and the Western Islands (Jura, Mull, and Skye).

The Lowlands encompass the entire Scottish mainland south of the Highlands except the Kintyre Peninsula where Campbeltown is located. Lowland malt whiskies are light bodied, relatively sweet, and delicate.

Islay is an island off the west coast. Traditional Islay malt whiskies are intensely smoky and pungent in character with a distinctive iodine or medicinal tang that is said to come from sea salt permeating the local peat that is used to dry the barley malt.

Campbeltown is a port located on the tip of the Kintyre Peninsula on the southwest coast that has its own distinctive spicy and salt-tinged malt whiskies.

IRELAND

A series of corporate consolidations and resulting plant closures have left the island with only three distilleries, one in County Antrim at the northern tip of Ulster, and two in the Republic of Ireland to the south. Several new and revised distilleries are, however, currently under construction.

JAPAN

The whisky distilleries of Japan are scattered throughout Honshu and Hokkaido, the two main northern islands of Japan, with the malt whisky distilleries located for the most part in mountainous regions where there are good water supplies.

NEW ZEALAND AND AUSTRALIA

New Zealand currently only has one operating whisky distillery in Dunedin, South Island. At press time, Australia had one operating whisky distillery in western Australia and three in Tasmania.

WHISKY COCKTAILS

SAZERAC

In a short glass combine:

- *2 ounces (60 ml) rye whiskey*
- *1 teaspoon (5 g) sugar*

Stir to blend, then add:

- *Dash Peychaud's bitters*
- *Dash Angostura bitters*
- *½ ounce (15 ml) Pernod*
- *2 ice cubes*

Stir to blend. Garnish with lemon twist.

DEPTH CHARGE

Fill a tall glass three-quarters full of beer. Pour 1 1/2 ounces (45 ml) Canadian whiskey into a shot glass. Drop the shot glass into the glass of beer and drink them together.

WHISKEY SOUR

Fill a short glass with ice. In a shaker combine:

- *1 ½ ounces (45 ml) blended whiskey*
- *1 ounce (30 ml) lemon juice*
- *1 tablespoon (15 g) sugar*
- *Crushed ice (half full)*

Shake and strain into the glass.

MANHATTAN

In a shaker combine:

- *1 ½ ounces (45 ml) bourbon*
- *¾ ounce (23 ml) sweet vermouth*
- *Ice*

Stir and strain into a martini (cocktail) glass or a short glass. Garnish with a maraschino cherry.

RUSTY NAIL

Fill a short glass with ice cubes. Add:

- *1 ounce (30 ml) Scotch whisky*
- *½ ounce (15 ml) Drambuie liqueur*

Stir and serve.

Sazerac Rye Whiskey

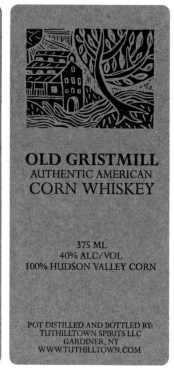

AMERICAN CORN WHISKEY

Tuthilltown Spirits Corn Whiskey is produced by the classic method, one batch at a time, from 100% Hudson Valley Corn. Known throughout the south as "white light'ning" or "moonshine", it is unaged to ensure you honest flavor and a traditional kick. Tuthilltown Corn Whiskey is a true American spirit. Enjoy it responsibly.

TuthillTown GRistMill
www.tuthilltown.com

GOVERNMENT WARNING: (1) ACCORDING TO THE SURGEON GENERAL, WOMEN SHOULD NOT DRINK ALCOHOLIC BEVERAGES DURING PREGNANCY BECAUSE OF THE RISK OF BIRTH DEFECTS. (2) CONSUMPTION OF ALCOHOLIC BEVERAGES IMPAIRS YOUR ABILITY TO DRIVE A CAR OR OPERATE MACHINERY, AND MAY CAUSE HEALTH PROBLEMS.

OLD GRISTMILL
AUTHENTIC AMERICAN
CORN WHISKEY

375 ML
40% ALC/VOL
100% HUDSON VALLEY CORN

POT DISTILLED AND BOTTLED BY:
TUTHILLTOWN SPIRITS LLC
GARDINER, NY
WWW.TUTHILLTOWN.COM

*Label for **Old Gristmill Authentic American Corn Whiskey** by **Tuthilltown Spirits***

John Henry

PipeLine Brand Agents, New York, New York

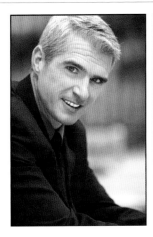

SUDDENLY, it is time to open the doors. You bought your still, got your license, built your distillery, sourced your raw products, decided what to make, and actually made some. The most important step is still ahead—you've got to convince people to buy what you're selling. Enter John Henry of PipeLine Brand Agents, a brand builder and market developer.

The task of reaching customers is daunting. Giant corporations can fly bevies of representatives around the world and ply retailers and restaurants with promotional wares, but the small distiller more often than not finds himself driving around in his own car with a case or two in the trunk. PipeLine's team of brand agents and market ambassadors are "dedicated to properly representing high-quality, artisanal spirits" (according to their website) and they work hard to build strong, supportive, mutually beneficial relationships.

"I tell the stories," said Henry. "Whether it is the history of a centuries-old brewery, the soil composition, the site and terroir of a sugarcane field or vineyard, or a cherished family recipe that goes back fourteen generations, I want to get out on the street and tell people about it."

Henry understands that a small distiller's product is a work of passion, and he wants to instill that passion in the marketplace and forge the sort of loyalty that can only be commanded by a craft product.

"I know the personalities, the history, and the drama. What's better than that? No corporate-created brand like 10 Cane has this history and rooted story."

Henry cuts a striking figure. He is a graduate of West Point and a former Army intelligence officer, but he left all that behind to ride his bicycle through the streets of New York, bottles clinking in his backpack.

"The bike is king. It's a story unto itself. It's green, it's street, it's artisanal, it moves. It's a hand-delivered, hand-sold way to do business, and I wouldn't have it any other way. I paraphrase Orwell: 'When I see a grown man on a bike, I have hope for the future.'"

Henry likes to say that he "farms relationships on the street—organically." In doing so, the hardest part of the job is also what makes it possible.

"What's most difficult about representing the more boutique, crafted brands is that you have to continually tell the story from scratch. The bigger brands bombard the consumer with images—think Vincent Gallo for Belvedere. With the smaller brands, you have to make the connection one on one as if you were the distiller, telling his story. That's what makes them stand out as brands and as distillers. I am as much a brand storyteller as I am a street-based brand builder. I look at my job as part Johnny Appleseed and part Johnny Carson."

CHAPTER FOUR

"The relationship between a Russian and a bottle of vodka is almost mystical."

— Richard Owen, British scientist and drinking buddy of Charles Darwin

VODKA

A colorful aray of craft vodkas on display, on ice, ready to be enjoyed responsibly

AS THE STORY goes, in 988, the Grand Prince of Kiev (Ukraine) decided it was time for his people to be converted from their pagan ways to one of the monotheistic religions that held sway to the south. First came the Jewish rabbis. He listened to their arguments, was impressed, but ultimately sent them away after noting that the followers of Judaism did not control any land. Next came the Muslim mullahs. Again he was impressed, both with their intellectual arguments and the success of Islam as a political and military force. But when he was told that Islam proscribed alcohol, he was dismayed and sent them away. Finally came the Christian priests, who informed him that not only could good Christians drink alcohol, but also that wine was required for church rituals such as communion. That was good enough for the Grand Prince, and on his command his subjects converted en masse to Christianity.

THE HISTORY OF VODKA

HISTORICALLY, the Slavic peoples of the north and their Scandinavian neighbors took alcoholic drinks very seriously. The extreme cold temperatures of winter inhibited the shipment of wines and beers, because these low-proof beverages could freeze during transit. Until the introduction of distilling into Eastern Europe in the 1400s, strong drink was made by fermenting wines, meads, and beers, freezing them, and then drawing off the alcoholic slush from the frozen water.

The earliest distilled spirit in Eastern Europe was made from mead (honey wine) or beer and was called *perevara*. The word *vodka* (from the Russian word *voda*, meaning "water") was originally used to describe grain distillates that were used for medicinal purposes. As distilling techniques improved, vodka (*wodka* in Polish) gradually came to be the accepted term for beverage spirit, regardless of its origin.

VODKA IN RUSSIA

Russians firmly believe that vodka was created in their land. Commercial production was established by the fourteenth century. In 1540, Czar Ivan the Terrible established the first government vodka monopoly. Distilling licenses were handed out to the boyars (the nobility), all other distilleries were banned, and moonshining became endemic.

Vodka production became an integral part of Russian society. Landowners operated stills on

Three Holstein stills

their estates and produced high-quality vodkas that were flavored with everything from acorns to horseradish to mint. The czars maintained test distilleries at their country palaces. In 1780, a scientist at one such distillery invented charcoal filtration to purify vodka.

By the eighteenth and into the nineteenth century, the Russian vodka industry was considered technologically advanced. New stills and production techniques from Western Europe were eagerly imported and utilized. State funding and control of vodka research continued. Under a 1902 law, "Moscow vodka," a clear 40 percent ABV rye vodka without added flavorings and soft "living" (undistilled) water, was established as the benchmark for Russian vodka.

The Soviet Union continued government control of vodka production. All distilleries became government-owned, and while the Communist Party apparatchiks continued to enjoy high-quality rye vodka, the proletariat masses had to make do with cheap spirits.

Vodka production in the current Russian Federation has returned to the pre-Revolutionary pattern. High-quality brands are again being produced for the new social elite and for export, while the popularly priced brands are still being consumed, well, like *voda*.

*Putting labels over the caps of freshly filled bottles of **Prezydent Vodka** at **Polmos Lodz** in Lodz, Poland*

those infused with small quantities of fruit spirit, being shipped throughout northern Europe and even into Russia.

With the fall of Communism in the late 1980s, the vodka distilleries soon returned to private ownership. Nowadays, high-quality Polish vodkas are exported throughout the world.

VODKA IN POLAND

The earliest written records of vodka production in Poland date from the 1400s, though some Polish historians claim that it was being produced around the southern city of Krakow at least a century earlier. Originally known as *okowita* (from the Latin *aqua vita*, "water of life"), it was used for a variety of purposes in addition to beverages. A 1534 medical text defined an aftershave lotion as "vodka for washing the chin after shaving." Herbal-infused vodkas were particularly popular as liniments for the aches and pains of life.

In 1546, King Jan Olbracht granted the right to distill and sell in spirits to every adult citizen. The Polish aristocracy, taking a cue from their Russian peers, soon lobbied to have this privilege revoked and replaced by a royal decree that reserved to them the right to make vodka.

Commercial vodka distilleries were well established by the eighteenth century. By the mid-nineteenth century, a thriving export trade had developed, with Polish vodkas, particularly

*Spirits dance in the still at the **Weyermann Distillery** in Bamberg, Germany.*

VODKA IN SWEDEN

Vodka production in Sweden, which dates from the fifteenth century, has its origins in the local gunpowder industry, where high-proof spirit (originally called *brännvin*) was used as a component of black powder for muskets. When distilleries were licensed to produce beverage alcohol (primarily spice-flavored aquavit, but also vodka), it was with the understanding that gunpowder makers had first priority over beverage consumers.

Home distilling was long a part of Swedish society. In 1830, there were more than 175,000 registered stills in a country of fewer than three million people. This tradition, in a much diminished and

VODKA AND THE CLASS SYSTEM

The societal attitude toward cheap spirits meant for the proletariat could be summed up by the curious fact that mass-produced vodka was sold in liter bottles with a non-screw cap. Once you opened the bottle, it couldn't be resealed. You had to drink it all in one session.

Charcoal filtration used in making vodka at **Colorado Pure Distilling**

illegal form, still continues to this day. Modern Swedish vodka is produced by the Vin & Sprit state monopoly.

VODKA IN THE UNITED STATES

Vodka was first imported into the United States in significant quantities around the turn of the twentieth century. Its market was immigrants from Eastern Europe. After the repeal of National Prohibition in 1933, the Heublein Company bought the rights to the Smirnoff brand of vodka from its White Russian émigré owners and relaunched vodka into the U.S. market. Sales languished until an enterprising liquor salesman in South Carolina started promoting it as "Smirnoff White Whisky—No taste. No smell." Sales boomed and American vodka, after marking time during World War II, was on its way to marketing success. The first popular vodka-based cocktail was a combination of vodka and ginger ale called the Moscow mule. It was marketed with its own special copper mug, examples of which can still be found on the back shelves of liquor cabinets throughout the United States

Today, vodka is the dominant white spirit in the United States, helped along by its versatility as a mixer and some very clever advertising campaigns. The most famous of these was the classic double entendre tagline: "Smirnoff—It leaves you breathless."

The majority of American craft distillers are vodka producers. They are divided between those who purchase neutral grain spirit (NGS) from a third party supplier and then rectify it in their own facility, and a relative handful of operations that produce and distill their own wash to make vodka. This is actually a serious challenge for craft distillers with pot stills, because it is difficult to produce a high-proof neutral grain spirit without using a column still.

The best-known, and best-selling, craft-distilled vodka is Tito's Handmade Vodka from the distillery of the same name in Austin, Texas.

THE BASIS OF VODKA

"A vodka martini, please. Polish, not Russian. Shaken, not stirred."

—James Bond, Agent 007, plunging
a stake into the heart of gin sales

VODKA is made by fermenting and then distilling the simple sugars from a mash of pale grain or vegetal matter, which can be potatoes, molasses, beets, or a variety of other plants. Rye is the classic grain for vodka, and most of the best Russian and Polish brands are made exclusively from a rye mash. Swedish and Baltic distillers are partial to wheat mashes, although wheat is also used farther east. Potatoes are looked down on by Russian distillers, but they are held in high esteem by some of their Polish counterparts. Molasses is widely used for inexpensive, mass-produced brands of vodka. American distillers use the full range of base ingredients.

DISTILLATION OF VODKA

Vodka is distilled in the manner described in the introductory chapter of this book. (See page 24.) The choice of pot or column stills does, however, have a fundamental effect on the final character of the vodka. All vodka comes out of the still as a clear, colorless spirit. But vodka from a pot still (the sort used for cognac and Scotch whisky) will contain some of the delicate aromatics, congeners, and flavor elements of the crop from which it was produced. Pot stills are relatively inefficient, and the resulting spirit from the first distillation is usually redistilled (rectified) to increase the proof of the spirit. Vodka from a more efficient column still is usu-

Local potatoes used in making vodka

ally a neutral, characterless spirit.

Except for a few minor exceptions, vodka is not put into wooden casks or aged for any extensive period of time. It can, however, be flavored or colored with a wide variety of fruits, herbs, and spices.

CLASSIFICATIONS OF VODKA

There are no uniform classifications of vodka. In Poland, vodkas are graded according to their degree of purity: standard (*zwykly*), premium (*wyborowy*), and deluxe (*luksusowy*). In Russia, vodka that is labeled osobaya (special) is usually a superior-quality product that

can be exported, while krepkaya (strong) denotes an overproof vodka of at least 56 percent ABV.

In the United States, domestic vodkas are defined by U.S. government regulation as "neutral spirits, so distilled, or so treated after distillation with charcoal or other materials, as to be without distinctive character, aroma, taste or color." Because American vodka is, by law, neutral in taste, there are only very subtle distinctions between brands. Many drinkers feel that the only real way of differentiating between them is by alcohol content and price.

VODKA REGIONS

EASTERN EUROPE

This is the homeland of vodka production. Every country produces vodka, and most also have local flavored specialties.

Russia, Ukraine, and Belarus produce the full range of vodka types, and they are generally acknowledged to be the leaders in vodka production. Only the better brands, all of which are distilled from rye and wheat, are exported to the West.

*Zubrowka vodka by **Polmos Bialystocka** is flavored with buffalo grass from the Bialowieza forest in Poland.*

FLAVORED VODKA

As a neutral spirit, vodka lends itself to blending with flavors and fortifying other beverages. In the nineteenth century, high-proof "Russian spirit" was held in high esteem by sherry producers in Spain, who imported it to fortify their wines. Neutral spirits are still used to fortify port, sherry, and other types of fortified wines, although the source of alcohol for such purposes these days tends to be the vast "wine lake" that has been created by European Union agricultural practices.

Flavored vodkas were originally used to mask the flavor of the first primitive vodkas, but they were later considered a mark of the distiller's skill. The Russians and Poles, in particular, still market dozens of flavors. Some of the better-known types are:

Kubanskaya: Vodka flavored with an infusion of dried lemon and orange peels

Limonnaya: Lemon-flavored vodka, usually with a touch of sugar added

Okhotnichya: "Hunter's" vodka is flavored with a mix of ginger, cloves, lemon peel, coffee, anise, and other herbs and spices. It is then blended with sugar and a touch of a wine similar to white port. It's a most unusual vodka.

Pertsovka: Pepper-flavored vodka, made with both black peppercorns and red chile peppers

Starka: "Old" vodka, a holdover from the early centuries of vodka production, which can be infused with everything from fruit tree leaves to brandy, port, Malaga wine, and dried fruit. Some brands are aged in oak casks.

Zubrovka: Zubrowka in Polish; vodka flavored with buffalo (or more properly "bison") grass, an aromatic grass favored by the herds of the rare European bison

In recent years, numerous flavored vodkas have been launched on the world market. The most successful of these have been fruit flavors, such as currant and orange.

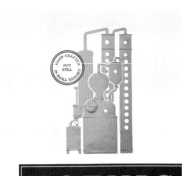

Poland produces and exports both grain- and potato-based vodkas. Most of the high-quality brands are produced in pot stills.

The Baltic States of Estonia, Latvia, and Lithuania, along with Finland, produce primarily grain-based vodkas, mostly from wheat.

WESTERN EUROPE

This region has local brands of vodka wherever there are distilleries. The base for these vodkas can vary from grains in northern countries, such as the United Kingdom, Holland, and Germany, to grapes and other fruits in the winemaking regions of France and Italy. Sweden has, in recent decades, developed a substantial export market for its straight and flavored wheat-based vodkas.

NORTH AMERICA

The United States and Canada produce vodkas, both from various grains (including corn) and from molasses. American vodkas are, by law, neutral spirits, so the distinction between nonflavored brands is more a matter of price and perception than taste. A number of flavored vodkas are also produced, both by the major distillers and by an assortment of craft distillers.

OTHER REGIONS

The Caribbean produces a surprising amount of vodka, all of it from molasses. Most of it is exported for blending and bottling in other countries.

Australia produces molasses-based vodkas, but few are exported.

Asia has a smattering of local vodkas, with the best coming from Japan.

Vermont White and Gold Vodka by Vermont Spirits

VODKA COCKTAILS

SCREWDRIVER

Fill a tall glass with ice. Add:

- *1 ½ ounces (45 ml) vodka*
- *Orange juice to fill*

Stir and serve.

BLOODY MARY

Fill a short glass with ice. Add:

- *1½ ounces (45 ml) vodka*
- *Dash Worcestershire sauce*
- *Dash Tabasco sauce*
- *Dash lemon or lime juice*
- *Tomato juice to fill*

Stir and garnish with celery salt on top.

SEX ON THE BEACH

Fill a tall glass with ice. Add:

- *1 ounce (30 ml) vodka*
- *1 ounce (30 ml) peach liqueur*
- *1 ½ ounces (45 ml) orange juice*
- *1 ½ ounces (45 ml) cranberry juice*

Stir and serve.

Mazama Infused Pepper Vodka by Bendistillery

ARTISAN PROFILE / INSIDE THE INDUSTRY

LeNell Smothers

Former owner of LeNell's, Brooklyn, New York

WHEN craft distillers Tuthill-town Spirits from Upstate New York launched their first barrel-aged whiskey, they called it Manhattan Rye, and they threw a party at the Four Season's Restaurant in the Seagrams Building on Park Avenue in Manhattan. In a big, open room, with bars at both ends and a mash of people laughing and drinking, they toasted their accomplishment and poured samples of their excellent whiskeys and vodkas (made from 100 percent New York State apples). When it came time to clink glasses and hear announcements, the crowd was treated to a raucous tutorial on mixing a Manhattan. Standing on a balcony above the crowd, like a hillbilly Juliet before a throng of devotees, LeNell Smothers cackled and cracked wise. She wore a battered cowboy hat, bandannas around her wrists, tight jeans, and a mile of attitude.

She took the crowd through the recipe: jigger of rye, shot of sweet vermouth, dash of bitters, shake, twist. She talked variation: The perfect Manhattan is half dry and half sweet vermouth. If they wanted to drink them on the rocks, do it. If they wanted to drink them straight up, go ahead. Do what you like, but do it with good booze.

Smothers moved from Alabama to New York City in 2000 and spent three years toiling in sales while her dream to open up a shop simmered. Her boutique wine and spirits shop in Red Hook, Brooklyn, opened in 2003. Red Hook is a rough, hip neighborhood on the waterfront, and her place fits right in. Small, eclectic, and very much driven by her personality, Smothers's store never wanted to have everything. For years, her vermouth selection was limited to one brand, Vya, the American vermouth made by Andy Quady of the Quady Winery in Madera, California, because it was made by a small producer.

Smothers was accepted into the bourbon community wholeheartedly, and her selection of American whiskey was breathtaking. When Jimmy Russell of Wild Turkey did a bottle signing in New York, he did it at her tiny shop.

Smothers, however tight she gets with the big producers, remains a champion of craft distilling. "When I go Charbay, I've got four generations of distillers there, hands on. Someplace like Stoli isn't going to have the same quality control."

Where some people call micro-distilling practices such as making 100 percent barley whiskeys or making whiskey from beer instead of from mash as controversial, Smothers believes that change and adventure are something to celebrate. "What is the American tradition anyway? All we do is our own thing."

In early 2009, after a trying struggle with her landlord, Smothers lost the lease to her shop. Next time, she's going to buy the building, she says, and expand the whiskey selection.

CHAPTER FIVE

"The proper union of gin and vermouth is a great and sudden glory; it is one of the happiest marriages on earth, and one of the shortest lived."

—Bernard DeVoto, American essayist and drinks philosopher

GIN

GIN is a juniper berry–flavored grain spirit. The word is an English shortening of genever, the Dutch word for juniper. The origins of gin are a bit murky. In the late 1580s, a juniper-flavored spirit of some sort was found in Holland by British troops who were fighting against the Spanish in the Dutch War of Independence. They gratefully drank it to give them what they soon came to call "Dutch courage" in battle. The Dutch themselves were encouraged by their government to favor such grain spirits over imported wine and brandy by lack of excise taxes on local drinks.

*This gooseneck still at **Philadelphia Distilling** was custom made by Forsyths of Scotland.*

THE HISTORY OF GIN

IN the 1600s, a Dr. Franciscus de la Boë in the university town of Leiden created a juniper- and spice-flavored medicinal spirit that he promoted as a diuretic. Genever soon found favor across the English Channel, first as a medicine (Samuel Pepys wrote in 1660 of curing a case of "colic" with a dose of "strong water made with juniper") and then as a beverage.

When the Dutch Protestant William of Orange became king of England in 1689, he moved to discourage the importation of brandy from the Catholic winemaking countries by setting high tariffs. As a replacement, he promoted the production of grain spirits ("corn brandy," as it was known at the time) by abolishing taxes and licensing fees for the manufacture of such local products as gin. History has shown that prohibition never works, but unfettered production of alcohol has its problems, too. By the 1720s, it was estimated that a quarter of the houses in London were used for the production or sale of gin. Mass drunkenness became a serious problem. The cartoonist Hogarth's famous depiction of such behavior in *Gin Lane* shows a sign above a gin shop that states, "Drunk for a penny/Dead drunk for twopence/Clean straw for Nothing." Panicky attempts by the government to prohibit gin production, such as the Gin Act of 1736, resulted in massive illicit distilling and the cynical marketing of "medicinal" spirits with such fanciful names as Cuckold's Comfort and My Lady's Eye Water.

A combination of reimposed government controls, the growth of high-quality commercial gin distillers, the increasing popularity of imported rum, and a general feeling of public exhaustion gradually brought this mass hysteria under control, although the problems caused by the combination of cheap gin and extreme poverty extended well into the nineteenth century. Fagin's irritable comment to a child in the film *Oliver*—"Shut up and drink your gin!"—had a basis in historical fact.

Wherever the British Empire went, English-style gins followed. In British colonies in North America, such celebrated Americans as Paul Revere and George Washington were notably fond of gin, and the Quakers were well known for their habit of drinking gin toddies after funerals.

The mid-nineteenth century ushered in a low-key rehabilitation of gin's reputation in England. The harsh, sweetened "Old Tom" styles of gin of the early 1700s slowly gave way to a new, cleaner style called dry gin. This style of gin became identified with the city of London to the extent that "London dry" became a generic term for the style, regardless of where it was actually produced.

Fritz Maytag, right, at **Anchor Distilling**. *With a small overhead crane, Achor Distilling can interchange the columns of their three stills.*

Bluecoat gin leaves the bottling line at **Philadelphia Distilling**.

Genteel middle-class ladies sipped their sloe gin (gin flavored with sloe berries) while consulting *Mrs. Beeton's Book of Household Management* (a wildly popular Victorian cross between the *Joy of Cooking* and Martha Stewart lifestyle books) for gin-based mixed drink recipes. The British military, particularly the officer corps, became a hotbed of gin consumption. Hundreds of gin-based mixed drinks were invented, and the mastery of their making was considered a part of a young officer's training. The best known of these cocktails, the gin and tonic, was created as a way for Englishmen in tropical colonies to take their daily dose of quinine, a very bitter medicine, to ward off malaria. (Modern tonic water still contains quinine, though as a flavoring rather than a medicine.)

BATHTUB GIN

Gin production in the United States dates back to Colonial times, but the great boost to gin production was the advent of National Prohibition in 1920. Moonshining quickly moved in to fill the gap left by the shutdown of commercial distilleries. But the furtive nature of illicit distilling worked against the production of the then-dominant whiskies, all of which required some aging in oak casks. Bootleggers were not in a position to store and age illegal whiskey, and the caramel-colored, prune-juice-dosed grain alcohol substitutes were generally considered to be vile.

Gin, on the other hand, did not require any aging, and it was relatively easy to make by

mixing raw alcohol with juniper berry extract and other flavorings and spices in a large container such as a bathtub (thus the origin of the term bathtub gin*). These gins were generally of poor quality and taste, a fact that gave rise to the popularity of cocktails in which the mixers served to disguise the taste of the base gin. Repeal of Prohibition at the end of 1933 ended the production of bootleg gin, but gin remained a part of the American beverage scene. It was the dominant white spirit in the United States until the rise of vodka in the 1960s. It still remains popular, helped along recently by the revived popularity of the martini.*

THE BASIS OF GIN

In Holland, the production of genever was quickly integrated into the vast Dutch trading system. Rotterdam became the center of genever distilling as distilleries opened there to take advantage of the abundance of needed spices that were arriving from the Dutch colonies in the East Indies (present-day Indonesia). Many of today's leading Dutch genever distillers can trace their origins back to the sixteenth and seventeenth centuries. Examples include such firms as Bols (founded 1575) and de Kuyper (1695).

Belgium developed its own juniper-flavored spirit, called jenever (with a j), in a manner similar to that in Holland (which controlled Belgium for a time in the early nineteenth century). The two German invasions of Belgium in World Wars I and II had a particularly hard effect on jenever producers as the occupying Germans stripped the distilleries of their copper stills and piping to use in the production of shell casings. The present-day remaining handful of Belgian jenever distillers produce primarily for the local domestic market.

Gin may have originated in Holland and developed into its most popular style in England, but its most enthusiastic modern-day consumers are to be found in Spain, which has the highest per capita consumption in the world. Production of London dry–style gin began in the 1930s, but serious consumption did not begin until the mix of gin and cola became inexplicably popular in the 1960s.

GIN and its Dutch cousin genever (jenever in Belgium) are white spirits that are flavored with juniper berries and so-called botanicals (a varied assortment of herbs and spices). The spirit base of gin is primarily grain (usually wheat or rye), which results in a light-bodied spirit. Genever is made primarily from "malt wine" (a mixture of malted barley, wheat, corn, and rye), which produces a fuller-bodied spirit similar to malt whisky. A small number of genevers in Holland and Belgium are distilled directly from fermented juniper berries, which produces a particularly intensely flavored spirit.

Bluecoat Gin by Philadelphia Distilling

The chief flavoring agent in both gin and genever is the highly aromatic blue-green berry of the juniper, a low-slung evergreen bush (genus *Juniperus*) that is commercially grown in northern Italy, Croatia, the United States, and Canada. Additional botanicals can include anise, angelica root, cinnamon, orange peel, coriander, and cassia bark. All gin and genever makers have their own secret combination of botanicals, the number of which can range from as few as four to as many as fifteen.

THE DISTILLATION OF GIN

Most gin is initially distilled in efficient column stills. The resulting spirit is high proof, light-bodied, and clean, with a minimal amount of congeners (flavor compounds) and flavoring agents. Genever is distilled in less-efficient pot stills, which results in a lower-proof, more flavorful spirit.

Low-quality "compound" gins are made by simply mixing the base spirit with juniper and botanical extracts. Mass-market gins are produced by soaking juniper berries and botanicals in the base spirit and then redistilling the mixture.

Top-quality gins and genevers are flavored in a unique manner. After one or more distillations, the base spirit is redistilled one last time. During this final distillation, the alcohol vapor wafts through a chamber in which the dried juniper berries and botanicals are

Guy Rehorst of the Great Lakes Distillery uses a wooden dipstick to measure the volume of spirit in a tank.

suspended. The vapor gently extracts aromatic and flavoring oils and compounds from the berries and spices as it travels through the chamber on its way to the condenser. The resulting flavored spirit has a noticeable degree of complexity.

THE COLORFUL ORIGINS OF OLD TOM GIN

The name of Old Tom Gin comes from what may be the first example of a beverage vending machine. In the 1700s, some pubs in England had a wooden plaque shaped like a black cat (an "Old Tom") mounted on the outside wall. Thirsty passersby would deposit a penny in the cat's mouth and place their lips around a small tube between the cat's paws. The bartender inside would then pour a shot of gin through the tube and into the customer's waiting mouth.

STYLE	DEFINITION	HOWEVER...
London Dry Gin	The dominant English style of gin in the United Kingdom, former British colonies, the United States, and Spain	It need not be truly "dry," and it lends itself well to mixing.
Plymouth Gin	Relatively full-bodied (compared to London dry gin). It is clear, slightly fruity, and very aromatic.	Originally the local gin style of Plymouth, England, modern Plymouth gin is made only by one distillery in Plymouth, Coates & Co., which also controls the right to the name Plymouth Gin.
Old Tom Gin	The last remaining example of the original lightly sweetened gins that were popular in eighteenth-century England	Limited quantities of Old Tom–style gin are still made by a few British distillers and several American craft distillers, but it is, at best, a curiosity item.
Genever or Hollands	The Dutch style of gin, distilled from a malted grain mash similar to that used for whiskey. Oude (old) genever is the original style. It is straw-hued, relatively sweet, and aromatic. Jonge (young) genever has a drier palate and lighter body. Some genevers are aged for one to three years in oak casks. Genevers tend to be lower proof than English gins (72 to 80 percent ABV is typical). They are usually served straight up and chilled.	The classic accompaniment to a shot of genever is a dried green herring. Genever is traditionally sold in a cylindrical stoneware crock. Genever-style gins are produced in Holland, Belgium, Germany, and the United States.

GIN REGIONS

Greylock Gin

EUROPE

The United Kingdom produces mostly dry gin, primarily from column stills. British gins tend to be high proof (90° proof or 45 percent ABV) and citrus-accented from the use of dried lemon and Seville orange peels in the mix of botanicals. British gins are usually combined into mixed drinks.

Holland and Belgium produce genever, mostly from pot stills. Genevers are distilled at lower proof levels than English gins and are generally fuller in body. Many of these gins are aged for one to three years in oak casks. Some genever producers now market fruit-flavored genevers, the best known being black currant. Dutch and Belgian genevers are usually chilled and served neat.

Germany produces a genever-style gin called dornkaat in the North Sea coast region of Frisia.

This spirit is lighter in body and more delicate in flavor than both Dutch genever and English dry gin. German gin is usually served straight up and cold.

Spain produces a substantial amount of gin, all of it in the London dry style from column stills. Most of it is sold for mixing with cola.

NORTH AMERICA

The United States is the world's largest gin market. London dry gin accounts for the bulk of domestic gin production, with most of it produced in column stills. American dry gins tend to be lower proof (80° proof or 40 percent ABV) and less flavorful than their English counterparts. This rule applies even to brands such as Gordon's and Gilbey's, which originated in England. The United States's best-selling gin,

*Label for **Genevieve** Genever style gin*

Bardenay London Style Dry Gin

Aviation Gin by House Spirits Distillery

Sarticious Gin by Sarticious Spirits

Seagram's Extra Dry, is a rare cask-aged dry gin. Three months of aging in charred oak barrels gives the gin a pale straw color and a smooth palate. American craft distilleries have taken to gin in a major way, with such noteworthy examples as Distiller's Gin #6 from North Shore Distillery in Lake Bluff, Illinois, and Rehorst Premium Milwaukee Gin from the Great Lakes Distillery in Milwaukee, Wisconsin.

THE MARTINI AND THE MEANING OF LIFE

The best known of hundreds of gin-based mixed drinks is the gin and white vermouth combination called the martini. As is usually the case with most popular mixed drinks, the origins of the martini are disputed. One school of thought holds that it evolved from the late-nineteenth-century martinez cocktail, a rather cloying mixture of Old Tom–style gin and sweet vermouth. A dissenting sect holds that it was created in the bar of the Knickerbocker Hotel in New York City in the early twentieth century. The ratio of gin to vermouth started out at about two to one, and it has been getting drier ever since. The famed British statesman Winston Churchill, who devoted a great deal of thought and time to drinking, was of the opinion that passing the cork from the vermouth bottle over the glass of gin was sufficient.

GIN COCKTAILS

CLASSIC MARTINI
In a shaker combine:
- *2 ounces (60 ml) gin*
- *Dash white vermouth*
- *Ice to fill*

Shake and strain and into a martini glass or a short glass. Garnish with an olive.

TOM COLLINS
In a tall glass combine:
- *2 ounces (60 ml) gin*
- *1 ounce (30 ml) lemon juice*
- *1 tablespoon (15 g) sugar*

Stir, and then fill the glass with ice. Fill with club soda.

GIN AND TONIC
Fill a tall glass with ice. Add:
- *1½ ounces (45 ml) gin*
- *Tonic water to fill*

Garnish with a lime slice.

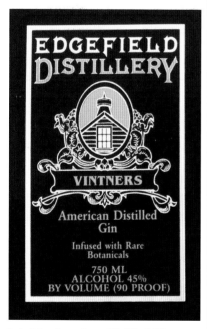

Label for **American Distilled Gin** *infused with Rare Botanicals by* **McMenamins Edgefield Distillery**

CHRIS WELD

Berkshire Mountain Distillers,
Great Barrington, Massachusetts

IT is hard to imagine Chris Weld in an emergency room, where he worked in California for sixteen years as a physician's assistant. He seems too young to have sixteen years of work behind him, and on his land in western Massachusetts, he is perfectly at ease with a dog at his side, light in his eyes, and mud on his boots.

He and his wife, Tyler, moved back to the East Coast—after having developed into serious foodies—and bought an orchard.

"Our water comes from an old spring here on the property that the *Pittsfield Sun* in 1901 said had 'few equals and none superior.'"

The farm that is now the Berkshire Mountain Distillery was once, in fact, a springwater bottling plant. (One former owner used it as a base of operations for a sanitarium in town, and it has also been a hotel.)

Building the Berkshire Mountain Distillery was not easy. When Weld arrived, the would-be still house was a barn in shambles. Weld did as much of the work as he could himself and hired local builders and craftspeople to do the rest. Keeping things local is important to Weld.

"When I need to expand, I'll build another barn, and I'll hire local people to build it." This implies a direct contrast to what happens when a big international distiller expands.

He talks enthusiastically about the "local multiplier" effect: "Every dollar you spend locally is worth three spent in a chain store."

Weld is an enthusiastic partici-

pant in the Berkshares program (local money accepted by hundreds of merchants in western Massachusetts, including restaurants). He hired a local designer to design labels. He sourced his glass out of nearby Lenox.

Weld looked further afield for help with his rum, and he brought in a consultant. Together they worked on test batches and perfected the recipe. He'd have worked for more than a year, he said, solving the problems that an expert solved in a few days, and the adjustments to fermentation temperatures and expert knowledge of different flavor compounds was priceless.

Weld describes his rum as more like Armagnac than a typical molasses distillate. He has fifty barrels aging.

"I've got a big still," he says. Indeed, he bought an 800-gallon stainless steel tank secondhand from Brown Foreman. (He assures anyone who asks that all the other work, including the custom columns and the piping, was done by local craftspeople.) "If I had a small still, I'd be at capacity." As it stands, he's able to make bourbon and rum for aging, bring out new products such as a second gin with a heavier flavor and more botanicals than his first, and still satisfy the 400 accounts he's developed in his first year.

For Weld, however, it's still the community that's important. He recently met into a man who had brought some of his Greylock Gin to a party. "Seeing it at parties . . . that's really it," he said, glowing.

CHAPTER SIX

"No sir, claret is the liquor for boys; port for men; but he who aspires to be a hero must drink brandy."

—Samuel Johnson, eighteenth-century British writer
who loved brandy and hated whisky

BRANDY AND EAU DE VIE

Brandy in a classic brandy snifter casts a shadow on a linen tablecloth.

THE word *brandy* comes from the Dutch word *brandewijn* (burnt wine), which is how the straightforward Dutch traders who introduced it to northern Europe in the sixteenth century described wine that had been "burnt," or boiled, to distill it.

The origins of brandy can be traced back to the growing Muslim Mediterranean states in the seventh and eighth centuries. Alchemists in the region experimented with distilling grapes and other fruits to make medicinal spirits. Their knowledge and techniques soon spread beyond the borders of the territory, with grape brandy production appearing in Spain and probably Ireland (via missionary monks) by the end of the eighth century.

Types of Brandy

BRANDY, in its broadest definition, is a spirit made from fruit juice or fruit pulp and skin. More specifically, it is broken down into three basic groupings.

Grape brandy is brandy distilled from fermented grape juice or crushed but not pressed grape pulp and skin. This spirit is aged in wooden casks (usually oak), which colors it, mellows out the palate, and adds aromas and flavors.

Pomace brandy (Italian *grappa* and French *marc* are the best-known examples) is made from the pressed grape pulp, skins, and stems that remain after the grapes are crushed and pressed to extract most of the juice for wine. Pomace brandies, which are usually minimally aged and seldom see wood, are an acquired taste. They often tend to be rather raw, although they can offer a fresh, fruity aroma of the type of grape used, a characteristic that is lost in regular oak-aged brandy.

Fruit brandy is the default term for all brandies that are made from fermenting fruit other than grapes. (It should not be confused with **fruit-flavored brandy**, which is grape brandy that has been flavored with the extract of another fruit.) Fruit brandies, except those made from berries, are generally distilled from fruit wines. Berries tend to lack enough sugar to make a wine with sufficient alcohol for proper distillation, and thus are soaked

Apples on the tree, raw materials for brandy

(macerated) in a high-proof spirit to extract their flavor and aroma. The extract is then distilled once at a low proof. **Calvados**, the apple brandy from the Normandy region of northwestern France, is probably the best-known type of fruit brandy. **Eau de vie** ("water of life") is a colorless fruit brandy, particularly from the Alsace region of France and from California.

Grapes enter the still for the making of grappa.

*A bottle of brandy distilled from 100 percent Viognier wine by **Germain-Robin***

Brandies by Region

France

French brandy is the catchall designation for brandy produced from grapes grown in other regions. These brandies are usually distilled in column stills and aged in oak casks for varying periods of time. They are frequently blended with wine, grape juice, oak flavorings, and other brandies, including cognac, to smooth out the rough edges. Cognac-like quality designations such as V.S.O.P. and Napoleon are often used (see page 83), but they have no legal standing.

Cognac

Cognac is the best-known type of brandy in the world, a benchmark by which most other brandies are judged. The Cognac region is located on the south-central coast of France, just north of Bordeaux, in the departments of Charente and Charente-Maritime. The region is further subdivided into six growing zones: Grande Champagne, Petite Champagne, Bois Ordinaries, Borderies, Fins Bois, and Bons Bois. The first two of these regions produce the best cognac and will frequently be so designated on bottle labels. The primary grapes used in making cognac are the Ugni Blanc, Folle Blanche, and Colombard. The wines made from these grapes are thin, tart, and low in alcohol, which are poor characteristics for table wines but perfect for making brandy.

Cognac is double distilled in specially designed pot stills and then aged in casks made from Limousin or Troncais oak. All cognacs start out in new oak to mellow the fiery spirit and give them color. Batches chosen for long-term aging are, after a few years, transferred to used, or "seasoned," casks that impart less of the oak flavor notes while the brandy matures.

Nearly all cognacs are a blend of brandies from different vintages and frequently different growing zones. Even those from single vineyards or distilleries have a mix of brandies from different casks. As with champagne, the products of local vineyards are sold to cognac houses, each of which stores and ages cognacs from different suppliers. The suppliers then employ master blenders to create and maintain continuity in the house blends drawn from disparate sources.

Brandy's Seasonal Nature

*Brandy, like rum and tequila, is an agricultural spirit. Unlike grain spirits such as whiskey, vodka, and gin, which are made throughout the year from grain that can be harvested and stored, brandy is dependent on the seasons, the ripening of the base fruit, and the production of the wine from which it is made. Types of brandies, originally at least, tended to be location-specific. (Cognac, for example, is a town and region in France that gave its name to the local brandy.) Important brandy-making regions, particularly in Europe, further differentiate their local spirits by specifying the types of grapes that can be used and the specific areas (**appellation**) in which the grapes used for making the base wine can be grown.*

Pear-in-bottle brandy

Barrels of brandy stored for aging

ARMAGNAC

Armagnac is the oldest type of brandy in France, with documented references to distillation dating back to the early fifteenth century. The Armagnac region is located in the heart of the ancient province of Gascony in the southwest corner of France. As with cognac, there are regional growing zones: Bas-Armagnac, Haut Armagnac, and Tenareze. The primary grapes used in making Armagnac are also the Ugni Blanc, Folle Blanche, and Colombard. But distillation takes place in the unique alambic armagnacais, a type of column still that is even more inefficient than a typical cognac pot still. The resulting brandy has a rustic, assertive character and aroma that requires additional cask aging to mellow out and distinguish it from cognac. The best Armagnac is aged in casks made from the local Monlezun oak. In recent years, Limousin and Troncais oak

INDUSTRY STANDARDS FOR COGNAC

Because there are no age statements on cognacs, the industry has adopted some generally accepted terms to differentiate cognacs. It is important to note that these terms have no legal status, and each cognac shipper uses them according to his or her own criteria.

V.S./V.S.P./Three Star: *(V.S.: very superior; V.S.P.: very superior pale) A minimum of two years aging in a cask, although the industry average is four to five years*

V.S.O.P.: *(very superior old pale) A minimum of four years' cask aging for the youngest cognac in the blend, with the industry average between ten and fifteen years*

X.O./Napoleon: *(X.O.: extra old) A minimum of six years' aging for the youngest cognac in the blend, with the average age running twenty years or older. All cognac houses maintain inventories of old vintage cognacs to use in blending these top-of-the-line brands. The oldest cognacs are removed from their casks in time and stored in glass demijohns (large jugs) to prevent further loss from evaporation and to limit excessively woody flavor notes.*

*Detail from a bottle of **Pierre Ferrand Reserve Cognac***

casks have been added to the mix of casks as suitable Monlezun oak becomes harder to find.

Most Armagnacs are blends, but unlike cognac, single vintages and single vineyard bottlings can be found. The categories of Armagnac are generally the same as those of cognac (V.S., V.S.O.P., X.O., and so on; see sidebar on page 83). Blended Armagnacs frequently have a greater percent-age of older vintages in their mix than comparable cognacs, making them a better value for the discerning buyer.

SPAIN

BRANDY DE JEREZ

Brandy de Jerez is made by the sherry houses centered around the city of Jerez de la Frontera in the southwest corner of Spain.

But virtually all Brandy de Jerez is made from wines produced elsewhere in Spain, primarily from the Airen grape in La Mancha and Extremadura, because the local sherry grapes are too valuable to divert into brandy production. Nowadays, most of the distilling is likewise done elsewhere in Spain in column stills. It is then shipped to Jerez for aging in used sherry casks in a solera system similar to that used for sherry wine. A *solera* is a series of large casks (called butts), each holding a slightly older spirit than the previous one beside it. When brandy is drawn off (racked) from the last butt (no more than a third of the volume

HAVE STILL, WILL TRAVEL

Until the 1970s, portable alambic armagnacais mounted on two-wheel carts were hauled among small vineyards in Armagnac by itinerant distillers called **bouilleurs de cru***. These traveling stills, alas, have mostly given way to larger fixed-in-place setups operated by farmer cooperatives and individual operators.*

Christian Drouin, *who produces some of the finest Calvados, stands beside a portable still built in 1946 that is now permanently stationed in front of the press-room at* **Domaine Coeur de Lion***. It is probably the only portable double distillation in working order. It is normally used from February to June. A second still now operates inside the pressroom.*

Brandy bottle detail from a brandy whose flavor profile leans more towards bourbon.

is removed), it is replenished with brandy drawn from the next butt all the way down the solera line to the first butt, where newly distilled brandy is added. This system of racking the brandy through a series of casks blends together a variety of vintages (some soleras have more than thirty stages) and results in a speeding up of the maturation process.

PENEDÈS BRANDY

Penedès Brandy is from the Penedès region of Catalonia in the northeast corner of Spain

AGING TIMELINE

Basic Brandy de Jerez Solera must age for a minimum of six months, Reserva for one year, and Gran Reserva for a minimum of three years.

In practice, the best Reservas and Gran Reservas are frequently aged for twelve to fifteen years. The lush, slightly sweet and fruity notes to be found in Brandy de Jerez come not only from aging in sherry casks but also from the judicious use of fruit-based flavor concentrates and oak essence (boise).

The sample bottles display the effects of different types of barrels and aging processes.

near Barcelona. Modeled after the cognacs of France and made from a mix of local grapes and the Ugni Blanc of cognac, it is distilled in pot stills. One of the two local producers (Torres) ages in soleras consisting of butts made from French Limousin oak, whereas the other (Mascaro) ages in the standard non-solera manner, but also in Limousin oak. The resulting brandy is heartier than cognac, but leaner and drier than Brandy de Jerez.

ITALY

Italy has a long history of brandy production dating back to at least the sixteenth century, but unlike Spain or France there are no specific brandy-producing regions. Italian brandies are made from regional wine grapes, and most are produced in column stills, although there are now a number of small artisanal producers using pot stills. They are aged in oak for a minimum of one to two years, with six to eight years being the industry average. Italian brandies tend to be on the light and delicate side with a touch of residual sweetness.

GERMANY

German monks were distilling brandy by the fourteenth century, and German distillers had organized their own guild as early as 1588. Yet almost from the start, German brandy (called *weinbrand*) has been made from imported wine rather than the more valuable local varieties. Most German brandies are produced in pot stills and must be aged for a minimum of six months in oak. Brandies that have been aged in oak for at least one year are called *uralt* or *alter* (meaning "older"). The best German brandies are smooth, somewhat lighter than cognac, and finish with a touch of sweetness.

The tasting room at a distillery is a popular stop on the tour.

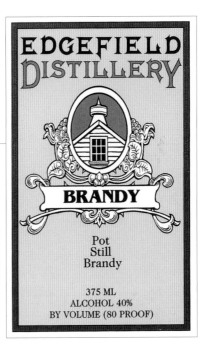

UNITED STATES

Grape brandy production in the United States, which until the advent of modern craft distilleries was mostly confined to California, dates back to the Spanish missions in the late eighteenth and early nineteenth centuries. A substantial amount of peach brandy was made by whiskey distillers in Southern states prior to National Prohibition, however, and apple brandy distilling continued into modern times on a modest scale in New Jersey and Virginia. In the years following the Civil War, brandy became a major industry, with a substantial export trade to Europe by the end of the nineteenth century. For a time, Leland Stanford, founder of Stanford University, was the world's largest brandy producer. Phylloxera and National Prohibition almost shut down the industry in the 1920s.

Repeal started things up again, but as with the bourbon industry, the advent of World War II resulted in brandy producers further marking time. Soon after the end of the war, the industry commissioned the University of California at Davis Department of Viticulture and Oenology to develop a prototype "California-style" brandy. It had a clean palate, was lighter in style than most European brandies, and had a flavor profile that made it a good mixer. Starting in the late 1940s, California brandy producers began to change over to this new style.

CONTEMPORARY BRANDIES

Contemporary commercial California grape brandies are made primarily in column stills from table grape varieties such as the Thompson Seedless and Flame Tokay. California brandies are aged for two to twelve years in used American oak (both brandy and bourbon casks) to limit woodiness in the palate, although pot distillers also use French oak. Several California distillers, most notably Korbel, have utilized the Spanish solera method for maturing their brandy. California brandies do not use quality designations such as V.S.O.P. or stars. The more expensive brands will usually contain a percentage of older vintages and pot-distilled brandies in the blend.

Craft-distilled brandies, including grape, pomace, and fruit, were the first of the modern generation of craft spirits to enter the U.S. market, starting in California in the late 1980s with producers such as RMS (a venture of

An alambic still

Pisco Style Brandy by **Leopold Bros.**

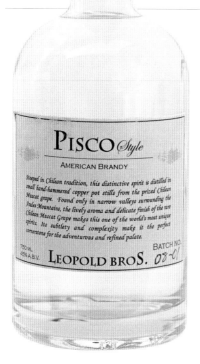

cognac producer Remy Martin), Jepson Vineyards, and the idiosyncratic Santa Cruz winemaker Randall Graham at Bonny Doone Vineyards. From the start, these grape brandy producers generally followed a French-themed muse, with producers such as Germaine-Robin in Mendocino County and Osocalis in the Santa Cruz Mountains going so far as to use the classic Ugni Blanc, Colombard, and Folle Blanche grapes to make their base wine. They installed special cognac-style pot stills to distill it, and then aged their brandies in casks made from imported Limousin or Troncais oak. The resulting brandies, particularly as longer-aged examples come on to the market, have, in some cases, shown levels of complexity and flavor intensity that put them on par with their European counterparts.

LATIN AMERICAN

MEXICO

In Mexico a surprising amount of wine is made, but it is little known outside of the country because most of it is used for brandy production. Mexican brandies are made from a mix of grapes, including the Thompson Seedless, Palomino, and Ugni Blanc. Both column and pot stills are used in production, whereas the solera system is generally used for aging. Brandy now outsells tequila and rum in Mexico.

SOUTH AMERICA

South American brandies are generally confined to their domestic markets. The best-known type is *pisco*, a clear, raw brandy from Peru and Chile that is made from Muscat grapes and double distilled in pot stills. The resulting brandy has a perfumed fragrance and serves as the base for a variety of mixed drinks, including the famous Pisco Punch.

OTHER REGIONS

Greece produces pot-distilled brandies, many of which, such as the well-known *Metaxa*, are flavored with Muscat wine, anise, or other spices.

Winemaking in Israel is a well-established tradition dating back thousands of years. But brandy production dates back only to the 1880s when the French Jewish philanthropist Baron Edmond de Rothschild established what has become the modern Israeli wine industry. Israeli brandy is made in the manner of cognac from Colombard grapes, with distillation in both pot and column stills and maturation in French Limousin oak casks.

In the Caucasus region, along the eastern shore of the Black Sea, the ancient nations of Georgia and Armenia draw on monastic traditions to produce rich, intensely flavored pot still brandies both from local grapes and from such imported varieties as the Muscadine (from France) and the Sercial and Verdelho (most famously from Madeira).

South Africa has produced brandies since the arrival of the first Dutch settlers in the seventeenth century, but these early spirits from the Cape Colony earned a reputation for being harsh firewater (*witblits*—white lightning—was a typical nickname). The introduction of modern production techniques and government regulations in the early twentieth century gradually led to an improvement in the quality of local brandies. Modern South African brandies are made from Ugni Blanc, Colombard, Chenin Blanc, and Palomino grapes, produced in both pot and column stills, and aged for a minimum of three years in oak.

POMACE BRANDIES

Oro de Mazzetti liqueur, gold suspended in a grappa base (Italy)

ITALY produces a substantial amount of grappa, both the raw, firewater variety and the more elegant, artisanal efforts that are made from one designated grape type and packaged in hand-blown bottles. Both types of grappa can be unaged or aged for a few years in old casks that will tame the hard edge of the spirit without imparting much flavor or color. Marc from France is produced in all of the nation's wine-producing regions, but it is mostly consumed locally. *Marc de Gewürztraminer* from Alsace is noteworthy because it retains some of the distinctive perfume nose and spicy character of the grape.

Craft pomace brandies from the United States, from producers such as Domaine Charbay in Napa County and Mosby Vineyards in Sonoma, are in the Italian style, and they are usually called grappas, even when they are made from non-Italian grape varieties. This is also true of the pomace brandies from Canada.

GRAPPA: NOT YOUR GRANDPA'S PHLEGM CUTTER

The U.S. government calls it pomace brandy, but ever since immigrants from winemaking countries began arriving in the United States and started to make wine, they were soon refermenting the pressed grape skins from their winemaking, and distilling it to make a quick and simple type of brandy. The French call it marc, but it is the Italian term grappa that has caught on with distillers of every ethnic background.

Craft distillers in the United States have taken to the distilling of grappa from the very start of the industry. Pioneer brandy distillers such as Clear Creek and St. George Spirits have developed specific varietal grappas that are carefully distilled to capture the subtle aromatic notes of the base fruit. These are spirits to delight the nose as much as the taste buds.

*Grappa by **Huber Starlight Distillery***

Poli Bassano del Grappa (Italy)

APPLE AND OTHER FRUIT BRANDIES

Eaux de vie bottles

NORMANDY is one of the few regions in **France** that does not have a substantial grape wine industry. Instead, it is apple country, with a substantial tradition of hard and sweet ciders that in turn can be distilled into an apple brandy known as *Calvados*. The local cider apples, which tend to be small and tart, are closer in type to crab apples than to modern table apples. This spirit has its own appellations, with the best brands coming from Appellation Controlee Pays d'Auge near the seaport of Deauville, and the rest in ten adjacent regions that are designated Appellation Reglementee. Most Pays d'Auge and some of the better Appellation Reglementee are produced in pot stills. All varieties of Calvados are aged in oak casks for a minimum of two years. Cognac-style quality and age terms such as V.S.O.P. and Hors d'Age are frequently used on labels, but have no legal meaning.

The fruit-growing regions of the upper Rhine River are the prime eau de vie production areas of Europe. The Black Forest region of Bavaria in Germany, and Alsace in France are known for their cherry brandies (*kir* in France, *kirschwasser* in Germany), raspberry brandies (*framboise* and *himbeergeist*), and pear brandies (*poire*). Similar eaux de vie are now being produced in the United States in California and Oregon. Some plum brandy is also made in these regions (*mirabelle* from France is an example), but the

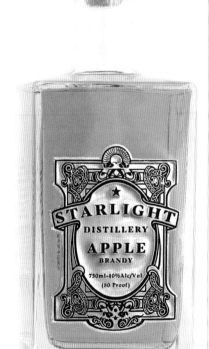

Apple brandy

*Exterior shot of **Laird & Company**, the oldest distillery in the United States*

best-known type of plum brandy is *slivovitz*, which is made from the small blue sljiva plum throughout Eastern Europe and the Balkans.

In the United States, *applejack*, as apple brandy is called locally, is thought by many to be the first spirit produced in the British colonies. This colonial tradition has continued with Laird's Distillery, established in 1780 in New Jersey and the oldest distilling company in the United States, and with distilleries in New Jersey and Virginia.

Artisan fruit brandy distilling started in California, but in recent years it has spread across the United States, with Calvados-styled apple brandies from Clear Creek Distillery in Portland, Oregon, leading the way, while Black Star Farms in Sutton Bay, St. Julian in Paw Paw, and a bevy of other Michigan artisan distillers have released a wide range of delicate, highly aromatic cherry, plum, and other fruit brandies that draw an obvious inspiration from the Kirsch and plum brandies of the Black Forest region of southern Germany.

BRANDY COCKTAILS

SIDECAR
Fill a short glass with ice. In a shaker combine:

- *1 ounce (30 ml) brandy*
- *1 ounce (30 ml) Triple Sec*
- *1 ounce (30 ml) lemon juice*
- *Ice to fill*

Shake and strain into the glass.

STINGER
Fill a short glass with ice. Add:

- *1 ounce (30 ml) brandy*
- *1 ounce (30 ml) white crème de menthe*

Stir and serve.

BRANDY ALEXANDER
In a shaker combine:

- *1 ounce (30 ml) brandy*
- *1 ounce (30 ml) dark crème de cacao*
- *1 ounce (30 ml) cream*
- *Ice to fill*

Shake and strain into a large brandy snifter. Dust with nutmeg.

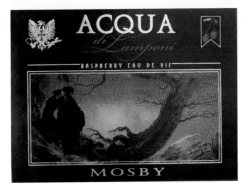

Label for **Acqua di Lamponi**, **Raspberry Eau de Vie**

CHAPTER SEVEN

*"There's nought no doubt so much the
spirit calms as rum and true religion."*

—Lord Byron

RUM, TEQUILA, LIQUEURS, AND MORE INCLUDING SCHNAPPS, ANISE, AND BITTERS

*Bottles of rum of different ages (youngest to oldest, left to right) at **Celebration Distillation** in New Orleans*

GRAPES AND GRAIN may be the two major raw materials for distillation, but they are by no means the only ones. Sugarcane provides two different fermentables: sugarcane juice and molasses, which is a byproduct of sugar refining. Both are used as the basis of rum production, which, as a spirit, ranges across the color and taste spectrum from the almost vodkalike Blancos of Puerto Rico to the hearty deep-hued Demeraras of Guyana, with some very distinctive variations in between.

RUM

The agave plant, a native of Central America, provides the fermentable basis for a variety of distilled spirits, of which tequila is the best known, but by no means the only example.

Liquors can refer generically to distilled spirits, but they can also be specifically flavored spirits. Add a sweetener, and they become liqueurs. Add certain herbs, and you now have bitters. At the end of the day, if something can be fermented and then distilled, people will drink it.

GROG

The British navy adopted a daily ration of a half-pint of 160° proof rum by the 1730s. This ration was subsequently modified by mixing it with an equal amount of water to produce a drink called grog. The grog ration remained a staple of British naval life until 1969.

THE HISTORY of rum is the history of sugar. Sugar is a sweet crystalline carbohydrate that occurs naturally in a variety of plants. One of those is the sugarcane (*Saccharum officinarum*), a tall, thick grass that has its origins in the islands of present-day Indonesia in the East Indies. Chinese traders spread its cultivation to Asia and on to India. Arabs in turn brought it to the Middle East and North Africa, where it came to the attention of Europeans during the Crusades in the eleventh century.

As the Spanish and Portuguese began to venture out into the Atlantic Ocean, they planted sugarcane in the Canary and Azores Islands. In 1493, Christopher Columbus picked up cane cuttings from the Canaries while on his second voyage to the Americas and transplanted them to Hispaniola, the Caribbean island now shared by Haiti and the Dominican Republic. Portuguese explorers soon did likewise in Brazil.

The Caribbean basin proved to have an ideal climate for growing sugarcane, and sugar production quickly spread around the islands. The insatiable demand in Europe for sugar soon led to the establishment of hundreds of sugarcane plantations and mills in the various English, Spanish, French, Portuguese, and Dutch colonies. These mills crushed the harvested cane and extracted the juice. Boiling this juice caused chunks of crystallized sugar to form. The remaining unsolidified juice was called *melazas* (from the Spanish word for honey, *miel*); in English this became molasses.

Molasses is a sticky syrup that still contains a significant amount of sugar. Sugar mill operators soon noticed that when it was

HUDSON RIVER RUM

375 ml   46% alc/vol
Pot Distilled From 100%
Blackstrap Molasses

PRODUCED AND BOTTLED
BY TUTHILLTOWN SPIRITS, GARDINER, NY
WWW.TUTHILLTOWN.COM

The character of HUDSON RIVER RUM is as rich and deep as the history of rum in the Northeastern US. Molasses shipped from the Islands was fermented and distilled in stills from the New England coast to Canada. Tuthilltown has produced a hearty rum with no doubt of its origin. We use heavy blackstrap molasses that leaves its mark on the nose and taste of this imposing spirit. Aged with American and European oak, River Rum is infused with the smokey feel of a northeastern night by the campfire. Try serving warm with a touch of cream to ward off the chill. We're happy to offer you this deliberate rum. It speaks for itself.

Year _____   Batch _____   Bottle _____

*Label for **Hudson River Rum** by **Tuthilltown Spirits***

*Prichard's Crystal Rum from **Prichards' Distillery***

*Prichard's Fine Rum from **Prichards' Distillery***

mixed with water and left out in the sun it fermented. By the 1650s this former waste product was being distilled into a spirit. In the English colonies it was called *Kill Devil* (from its tendency to cause a nasty hangover or its perceived medicinal power, take your choice) or *rumbullion* (origins uncertain), which was shortened over the years to our modern word *rum*. The French render this word as *rhum*, while the Spanish call it *ron*.

Rum was used as a cure-all for many of the aches and pains that afflicted those living in the tropics. Sugar plantation owners sold it, at discounted prices, to naval ships that were on station in the Caribbean in order to encourage their presence in local waters and thus discourage the attentions of marauding pirates.

This naval-rum connection introduced rum to the outside world, and by the late seventeenth century a thriving export trade developed. The British islands shipped rum to Great Britain (where it was mixed into rum punches and replaced gin as the dominant spirit in the eighteenth century) and to the British colonies in North America, where it became very popular. This export of rum to North America, in exchange for New England lumber and dried cod (still a culinary staple in the Caribbean), soon changed over to the export of molasses to distilleries in New England. This was done to avoid

*Bob Ryan and partner **Dave Wood** at **Ryan and Wood Distilleries** in Gloucester, Massachusetts.*

Dark Rum, Spruce Gin, White Rum, and Hazelnut Spice Rum by Rogue Distillery

laws from the British parliament, which protected British distillers by forbidding the trade in spirits directly between colonies. This law was, at best, honored in the breech, and smuggling soon became rampant.

The shipping of molasses to make rum in New England distilleries became part of the infamous "slavery triangle." The first leg was the shipment of molasses to New England to make rum. The second leg was the shipment of rum to the ports of West Africa to trade for slaves. The final leg was the passage of slave ships to the sugar plantations of the Caribbean and South America, where many of the slaves were put to work in the sugarcane fields.

The disruption of trade caused by the American Revolution and the rise of whiskey production in North America resulted in the slow decline of rum's dominance as the American national tipple. Rum production in the United States slowly declined through the nineteenth century, with the last New England rum distilleries closing at the advent of National Prohibition in 1920. The famed rumrunners of the Prohibition era were smuggling primarily whiskey into the United States.

In Europe, the invention of sugar extraction from the sugar beet lessened the demand for Caribbean sugar, reducing the amount of molasses being produced and the resulting amount of rum being distilled. Many small plantations and their stills were closed. Rum production receded,

STYLE	DEFINITION
White Rums	Generally light-bodied (although there are a few heavy-bodied white rums in the French islands). They are usually clear and have a very subtle flavor profile. If they are aged in oak casks to create a smooth palate, they are then usually filtered to remove any color. White rums are primarily used as mixers and blend particularly well with fruit flavors.
Golden Rums	Also known as amber rums, these are generally medium-bodied. Most have spent several years aging in oak casks, which give them smooth, mellow palates.
Dark Rums	Traditionally, full-bodied, rich caramel-dominated rums, the best are produced mostly from pot stills and frequently aged in oak casks for extended periods. The richest of these rums are consumed straight up.
Spiced Rums	White, golden, or dark rums, they are infused with spices or fruit flavors. Rum punches (such as planter's punch) are blends of rum and fruit juices that are very popular in the Caribbean.
Age-Dated Blended Rums	These are aged rums from different vintages or batches that are mixed together to ensure a continuity of flavor in brands of rum from year to year. Some aged rums will give age statements stating the youngest rum in the blend (e.g., a ten-year-old rum contains a blend of rums that are at least ten years old). A small number of French island rums are vintage dated.

Chris Weld of *Berkshire Mountain Distillers*

gnacs, and small-batch bourbons, who are learning to appreciate the subtle complexities of these rums. The pot still rums of Guyana and Jamaica have a particular appeal for Scotch whisky drinkers. (It is no accident that the Scottish whisky merchant and bottler Cadenhead also ages and bottles Demerara rum.) The subtle and complex *rhums* of Martinique and Guadeloupe mirror the flavor profiles of the top French brandies in Cognac and Armagnac.

THE BASIS OF RUM

Rum, and its fraternal twin, cane spirit, are made by distilling fermented sugar and water. This sugar comes from the sugarcane and is fermented from cane juice, concentrated cane juice, or molasses. Molasses is the sweet, sticky residue that remains after sugarcane juice is boiled and the crystallized sugar is extracted.

Most rum is made from molasses. Molasses is more than 50 percent sugar, but it also contains significant amounts of minerals and other trace elements, which can contribute to the final flavor. Rums made from cane juice, primarily on Haiti and Martinique, have a naturally smooth palate.

Depending on the recipe, the "wash" (the cane juice, or molasses and water) is fermented, using either cultured yeast or airborne wild yeasts, for a period ranging from twenty-four hours for light rums up to several weeks for heavy, full varieties.

for the most part, to countries where sugarcane was grown.

The modern history of rum owes a lot to the spread of air-conditioning and the growth of tourism. In the second half of the twentieth century, modern air-conditioning made it possible for large numbers of people to migrate to warm-weather regions where rum remained the dominant spirit. Additionally, the explosive increase in the number of North American and European tourists into rum-drinking regions led to a steady increase in the popularity of rum-based mixed drinks. Nowadays, white rum gives vodka serious competition as the mixer of choice in a number of distinctively nontropical markets.

Aged rums are gaining new standing among consumers of single malt Scotch whiskies, co-

Old New Orleans Crystal Rum by Celebration Distillation

*Coaster for **Ragged Mountain Rum** by **Berkshire Mountain Distillers**: "Think Globally, Drink Locally"*

DISTILLATION OF RUM

Rum can be distilled in either pot or column stills. The choice of stills has a profound effect on the final character of the rum. All rums come out of the still as clear, colorless spirits. Barrel aging and the use of added caramel determine the final color. Because caramel is burnt sugar, it is true that only natural coloring agents are used.

Lighter rums are highly rectified (purified) and are produced in column or continuous stills, then usually charcoal filtered and sometimes aged in old oak casks for a few months to add smoothness. Most light rums have minimal flavors and aroma and are very similar to vodka. Heavier rums are usually distilled in pot stills, similar to those used to produce cognacs and Scotch whiskies. Pot stills are less efficient than column stills and some congeners (fusel oils and other flavor elements) are carried over with the alcohol. These heavier rums are used for making golden and dark rums.

Some brands of rum are made by blending pot- and column-distilled rums in a manner similar to that of Armagnac production.

RUM COCKTAILS

RUM AND COKE (Cuba Libre)
Fill a tall glass with ice. Add:

- *1 ½ ounces (45 ml) dark rum*
- *Juice of half a lime*
- *Cola to fill*

Stir and garnish with a lime wedge.

DAIQUIRI

Fill a short glass with ice. In a shaker combine:

- *1 ½ ounces (45 ml) white rum*
- *1 ounce (30 ml) lime juice*
- *1 tablespoon (15 g) sugar*
- *Ice to fill*

Shake and strain into the glass.

PLANTER'S PUNCH

Fill a tall glass with ice. In a shaker combine:

- *1 ½ ounces (45 ml) dark rum*
- *½ ounce (15 ml) lime juice*
- *½ ounce (15 ml) lemon juice*
- *3 ounces (90 ml) orange juice*
- *1 teaspoon (5 g) sugar*
- *Dash grenadine syrup*
- *Ice to fill*

Shake and strain into the glass.

Sagatiba Pura Cachaça (Brazil)

RUM REGIONS

THE CARIBBEAN

The Caribbean is the epicenter of world rum production. Virtually every major island group produces its own distinct rum style.

Barbados produces light, sweetish rums from both pot and column stills. Rum distillation began here, and the Mount Gay Distillery, dating from 1663, is probably the oldest operating rum producer in the world.

Cuba produces light-bodied, crisp, clean rums from column stills. It is currently illegal to ship Cuban rums into the United States.

The Dominican Republic is notable for its full-bodied, aged rums from column stills.

Guyana is justly famous for its rich, heavy Demerara rums, named for a local river, which are produced from both pot and column stills. Demerara rums can be aged for extended periods (twenty-five-year-old varieties are on the market) and are frequently used for blending with lighter rums from other regions. Neighboring Surinam and French Guyana produce similar full-bodied rums.

Haiti follows the French tradition of heavier rums that are double distilled in pot stills and aged in oak casks for three or more years to produce full-flavored, exceptionally smooth-tasting rums. Haiti also still has an extensive underground moonshine industry that supplies the voodoo religious ritual trade.

Jamaica is well known for its rich, aromatic rums, most of which are produced in pot stills. Jamaica has official classifications of rum, ranging from light to very full-flavored. Jamaican rums are used extensively for blending.

Martinique is a French island with the largest number of distilleries in the Eastern Caribbean. Both pot and column stills are used. As on other French islands such as Guadeloupe, both *rhum agricole* (made from sugarcane juice) and *rhum industriel* (made from molasses) are produced. These rums are frequently aged in used French brandy casks for a minimum of three years. *Rhum vieux* (aged rum) is frequently compared to high-quality French brandies.

Puerto Rico is known primarily for light, very dry rums from column stills. All Puerto Rican rums must, by law, be aged for a minimum of one year.

Trinidad produces mainly light rums from column stills and has an extensive export trade.

THE VIRGIN ISLANDS

The Virgin Islands, which are divided between the United States Virgin Islands and the British Virgin Islands, both produce light, mixing rums from column stills. These rums, and those of nearby Grenada, also serve as the base for bay rum, a classic aftershave lotion.

CENTRAL AMERICA

Central America has a variety of primarily medium-bodied rums from column stills that lend them-

*Distiller **Stefan Hafen** at the **Weyermann Distillery** (Germany)*

selves well to aging. They have recently begun to gain international recognition.

SOUTH AMERICA

South America produces vast quantities of mostly light rums from column stills, with unaged cane spirit from Brazil, called *cachaça*, being the best-known example. Venezuela bucks this general trend with a number of well-respected barrel-aged golden and dark rums.

NORTH AMERICA

North America has a handful of traditional rum distilleries in the southern United States, producing a range of light- and medium-bodied rums that are generally marketed with Caribbean-themed names. Modern craft distilleries producing rum have sprung up in some more unusual locations, with particularly noteworthy producers including Prichard's Distillery in Kelso, Tennessee; the Rogue Distillery in Newport, Oregon; and the Triple 8 Distillery in Nantucket, Massachusetts.

CANADA

In Canada the 300-year-old tradition of trading rum for dried codfish continues in the Atlantic Maritime provinces of Newfoundland and Nova Scotia, where golden rums from Antigua, Barbados, and Jamaica are imported and aged for five years. The resulting hearty rum is known locally as *screech*.

EUROPE

Europe is primarily a blender of imported rums. Both the United Kingdom and France import rums from their former colonies in the Caribbean for aging and bottling. Heavy, dark Jamaican rums are imported into Germany and mixed with neutral spirit at a 1:19 ratio to produce *rum verschnitt*. A similar product in Austria is called *inlander rum*.

AUSTRALIA

Australia produces a substantial amount of white and golden rums in a double-distillation method utilizing both column and pot stills. Rum is the second most popular alcoholic beverage in the country after beer. Light rums are also produced on some of the islands in the South Pacific such as Tahiti.

ASIA

In Asia, rums tend to follow regional sugarcane production, with white and golden rums from column stills being produced primarily in the Philippines and Thailand.

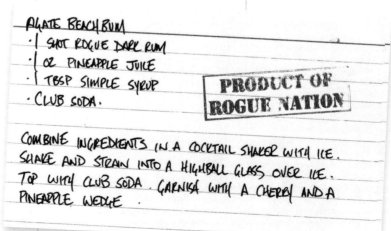

AGATE BEACH RUM
- 1 SHOT ROGUE DARK RUM
- 1 OZ PINEAPPLE JUICE
- 1 TBSP SIMPLE SYRUP
- CLUB SODA.

PRODUCT OF ROGUE NATION

COMBINE INGREDIENTS IN A COCKTAIL SHAKER WITH ICE. SHAKE AND STRAIN INTO A HIGHBALL GLASS OVER ICE. TOP WITH CLUB SODA. GARNISH WITH A CHERRY AND A PINEAPPLE WEDGE.

*Recipe card from **Rogue Distillery***

Tequila, Mezcal, and Other Agave Spirits

TEQUILA, its sister spirit mezcal, and other agave spirits trace their origins back at least 2,000 years to when one or more of the Indian tribes that inhabited what is now central Mexico discovered that the juice of the agave plant, if left exposed to air, would ferment and turn into a milky, mildly alcoholic drink. News of this discovery spread throughout agave-growing areas. The Aztecs called this beverage *octili poliqhui*, a name that the Spaniards subsequently corrupted into *pulque* (POOL-kay).

In Aztec culture, pulque drinking had religious significance. Consumption by the masses was limited to specific holidays, when large tubs of pulque were set up in public squares. The ruling elite was not subject to the same restrictions, however, and drank pulque throughout the year—a privilege shared by captive warriors just before they were sacrificed to the gods.

When the Spanish arrived in Mexico in the early sixteenth century, they soon began to make and drink pulque. But the low alcohol content (around 3 percent ABV) and earthy, vegetal taste made it less popular among the conquistadors than European-style beers and brandies. Early attempts to distill pulque were unsuccessful, and the resulting spirit was harsh and acrid. It was soon discovered, however, that cooking the agave pulp resulted in a sweeter juice that, when fermented, became known as mezcal wine. This "wine" was then distilled into the spirit that we know today as mezcal.

Early mezcal distilleries in the Spanish colony of Mexico operated in a manner similar to modern-day brewpubs. The distilling plant was usually small, and its production was consumed primarily in the distillery tavern (*taberna*). As the colony grew, the mezcal wine industry followed apace and soon became an important source of tax

Blue agave, the raw material for tequila and mezcal

revenue for the Crown. Periodic attempts by Spanish brandy producers to shut down the mezcal industry were about as unsuccessful as similar efforts by English distillers to inhibit rum production in the British colonies in North America.

THE EVOLUTION OF TEQUILA

In 1656, the village of Tequila (named for the local Ticuilas Indians) was granted a charter by the governor of New Galicia. Tax records of the time show that mezcal was already being produced in the area. This mezcal, made from the local blue agave, established a reputation for having a superior taste, and barrels of the "mezcal wine from Tequila" were soon being shipped to nearby Guadalajara and more distant cities such as the silver-mining boomtowns of San Luis Potosí and Aguascalientes.

The oldest of the still-existing distilleries in Tequila dates back to 1795, when the Spanish Crown granted a distiller's license to Jose Cuervo. In 1805, a distillery was established that would ultimately come under the control of the Sauza family. By the mid-1800s, there were dozens of distilleries and millions of agave plants under cultivation around Tequila in what had become the state of Jalisco. Gradually, the locally produced mezcal came to be known as tequila (just as the grape brandy from the Cognac region in France came to be known simply as cognac).

A jimador harvests blue agave for making tequila in Jalisco, Mexico.

Mexico achieved independence from Spain in 1821. But until the 1870s it was a politically unstable country that experienced frequent changes in government, revolutions, and a disastrous war with the United States. Marauding bands of soldiers and *guerillas* extracted "revolutionary taxes" and "voluntary" contributions in kind from the tabernas and distilleries. In 1876 a general named Porfirio Díaz, who was from the mezcal-producing state of Oaxaca (oah-HA-kuh), came to power and ushered in a thirty-five-year period of relative peace and stability known as the *Porfiriato*.

It was during this period that the tequila industry became firmly established. Modest exports of tequila began to the United States and Europe, with Jose Cuervo shipping the first three barrels to El Paso, Texas, in 1873. By 1910 the number of agave distilleries in the state of Jalisco had grown to almost a hundred.

The collapse of the Díaz regime in 1910 led to a decade-long period of revolution that inhibited the tequila industry. The return of peace in the 1920s led to the expansion of tequila production in Jalisco beyond the area around the town of Tequila, with growth being particularly noteworthy in the highlands around the village of Arandas. This period also saw the adoption of modern production techniques from the wine industry, such as cultivated yeast and microbiological sanitary practices.

In the 1930s, the practice of adding non-agave sugars to the *aguamiel*, or "honey water," was introduced and quickly adopted by many tequila producers. These *mixto* (mixed) tequilas had a less intense taste than 100 percent blue agave tequilas. But this relative blandness also made them more appealing to nonnative consumers, particularly those in the United States.

THE BASIS OF TEQUILA AND MEZCAL

Tequila and mezcal are made by distilling the fermented juice of agave plants in Mexico. The agave is a spiky-leafed member of the lily family (it is not a cactus) and is related to the century plant. By Mexican law, the agave spirit called tequila can be made only from one particular type of agave, the blue agave (*Agave tequilana Weber*), and it can be produced only in specifically designated geographic areas, primarily the state of Jalisco in west-central Mexico. Mezcal is made from the

fermented juice of other species of agave. It is produced throughout most of Mexico.

Both tequila and mezcal are prepared for distillation in similar ways. The agave, also know as maguey (pronounced muh-GAY), is cultivated on plantations for eight to ten years, depending on the type of agave. When the plant reaches sexual maturity, it starts to grow a flower stalk. The agave farmer, or *campesino*, cuts off the stalk just as it is starting to grow. This redirects the plant growth into the central stalk, swelling it into a large bulbous shape that contains a sweet juicy pulp. When the swelling is completed, the campesino cuts the plant from its roots and removes the long sword-shaped leaves, using a razor-sharp pike-like tool called a *coa*. The remaining piña ("pineapple"—so-called because the cross-thatched denuded bulb resembles a giant green and white pineapple) weighs anywhere from twenty-five to one hundred pounds.

At the distillery, the piñas are cut into quarters. For tequila, they are then slowly baked in steam ovens or autoclaves until all of the starch has been converted to sugars. For mezcal, they are baked in underground ovens heated with wood charcoal (which gives mezcal its distinctive smoky taste). They are then crushed (tradition-

ally with a stone wheel drawn around a circular trough by a mule) and shredded to extract the sweet juice, called *aguamiel* (honey water).

FERMENTATION: AGAVE OR MIXTO

The fermentation stage determines whether the final product will be 100 percent agave or mixed ("mixto"). The highest-quality tequila is made from fermenting and then distilling just agave juice mixed with some water. Mixto is made by fermenting and then

WHAT BING CROSBY AND JIMMY BUFFETT HAVE IN COMMON

Modest amounts of tequila had been exported into U.S. border towns since the late nineteenth century. The first major boost to tequila sales in the United States came in the late 1940s when the margarita cocktail, a blend of tequila, lime juice, orange liqueur, and ice, was invented. Its origins are uncertain, but Hollywood actors and cocktail parties in California and Mexican resorts seem to be involved in most of the genesis stories. It is known that crooner and actor Bing Crosby was so taken with one particular brand of tequila, Herradura, that he teamed up with fellow actor Phil Harris to import the brand into the United States. The margarita, along with the tequila sunrise and the tequila sour, have become highly popular in the United States; in fact, it is claimed by many in the liquor industry that the margarita is the single most popular cocktail in the nation. In the 1970s, when balladeer Jimmy Buffett sang of "wasting away in Margaritaville," the success of the song enticed millions more Americans to sip from the salt-rimmed margarita glass.

Stills used for producing tequila

distilling a mix of agave juice and other sugars, usually cane sugar with water. Mixtos made and bottled in Mexico can contain up to 40 percent alcohol made from other sugars. Mixtos that have been shipped in bulk to other countries for bottling (primarily the United States) may have the agave content further reduced to 51 percent by the foreign bottler. By Mexican law, all 100 percent agave or aged tequilas must be bottled in Mexico. If a tequila is 100 percent agave, it will always say so on the bottle label. If it doesn't say 100 percent, it is a mixto, although that term is seldom used on bottle labels.

DISTILLATION AND AGING OF TEQUILA AND MEZCAL

Traditionally, tequila and mezcal have been distilled in pot stills at 110° proof (55 percent ABV). The resulting spirit is clear but contains a significant amount of congeners and other flavor elements. Some light-colored tequilas are now being rectified (redistilled) in column stills to produce a cleaner, blander spirit.

Color in tequila and mezcal comes mostly from the addition of caramel, although barrel aging is a factor in some high-quality brands. Additionally, some distillers add small amounts of natural flavorings such as sherry, prune concentrate, and coconut to manipulate the product's flavor profile. These added flavors do not stand out themselves, but instead

THE BLUE AGAVE STRIKES BACK

From the 1930s through the 1980s, the bulk of the tequila being produced was of the blended mixto variety. The original 100 percent agave tequilas were reduced to a minor specialty product in the market. In the late 1980s, the rising success of single malt Scotch whiskies and expensive cognacs in the international marketplace did not go unnoticed among tequila producers. New brands of 100 percent blue agave tequilas were introduced, and sales began a steady growth curve that continues to this day.

CLASSIFICATIONS OF TEQUILA

Beyond the two basic designations of tequila—agave and mixto—there are four categories:

STYLE	DEFINITION	HOWEVER...
Silver or **Blanco**	Clear, with little (no more than sixty days in stainless steel tanks) or no aging. They can be either 100 percent agave or mixto. Silver tequilas are used primarily for mixing and blend particularly well into fruit-based drinks.	Once you have confirmed that it is 100 percent blue agave, a fancy bottle and a higher price do not necessarily mean that it is a better spirit.
Gold	Unaged silver tequila that has been colored and flavored with caramel. It is usually a mixto.	A product category produced primarily for silly gringos. Serious tequila drinkers go for reposados.
Reposado/ Rested	"Rested" tequila is aged in wooden tanks or casks for a legal minimum period of at least two months, with the better-quality brands spending three to nine months in wood. It can be either 100 percent agave or mixto.	Reposado tequilas are the best-selling tequilas in Mexico.
Añejo/Aged	"Old" tequila is aged in wooden barrels (usually old bourbon barrels) for a minimum of twelve months. The best-quality anejos are aged for eighteen months to three years for mixtos, and up to four years for 100 percent agaves.	Aging tequila for more than four years is a matter of controversy. Most tequila producers oppose doing so because they feel that "excessive" oak aging will overwhelm the distinctive earthy and vegetal agave flavor notes.

Barrels set for aging tequila in a warehouse/tasting room

serve to smooth out the often hard-edged palate of agave spirit.

MEZCAL AND THE WORM

The rules and regulations that govern the production and packaging of tequila do not apply to agave spirits produced outside of the designated areas in Mexico. Some mezcal distilleries are very primitive and very small. The best-known mezcals come from the southern state of Oaxaca, although they are produced in a number of other states. Eight varieties of agave are approved for mezcal production, but the chief variety used is the espadin agave (*Agave angustifolia Haw*).

The famous "worm" found in some bottles of mezcal (*"con gusano"*) is the larva of one of two moths that live on the agave plant. The reason for adding the worm to the bottle of mezcal is obscure. But one story, which at least has the appeal of logic to back it up, is that the worm serves as proof of high proof: the worm remains intact in the bottle if the percentage of alcohol in the spirit is high enough to preserve the pickled

AS THE WORM TURNS

The upgrading and upscaling of tequila has, in turn, inspired mezcal producers to undertake similar measures. In the past few years, an increasing number of high-end mezcals, including some intriguing "single village" bottlings, have been introduced to the market. Mezcal now seems to be coming into its own as a distinctive, noteworthy spirit.

A bottle of **Agua Azul**, a blue agave eau de vie

Brendan Moylan holds up a couple of bottles of **JB Wagoner's 100 percent Blue Agave Spirits** in front of his well-stocked bar.

worm. Consuming the worm, which can be done without harm, has served as a rite of passage for generations of fraternity boys. Top-quality mezcals do not include a worm in the bottle.

NON-MEXICAN AGAVE SPIRITS

Federal excise tax records indicate that tequila-like agave spirits were produced in the 1930s in the southwestern United States. More recently, modern craft distillers have begun to experiment with their own agave spirits, such as JB Wagoner's Ultra Premium 100 percent Blue Agave Spirits by Skyrocket Distillers in Temucula, California; Agua Azul by St. George Spirits in Alameda, California; and Gold Agave by St. James Spirits in Irwindale, California.

TEQUILA COCKTAILS

CLASSIC MARGARITA

Take a short glass. Wet the rim with lime juice. Put the glass upside down in coarse salt, so that the salt clings to the rim. In a cocktail shaker combine:

- 1 ½ ounces (45 ml) silver tequila
- ¾ ounce (23 ml) Triple Sec
- ¾ ounce (23 ml) lime juice
- Ice to fill

Shake and strain into the salt-rimmed glass and garnish with a lime slice.

FROZEN FRUIT MARGARITA

Take a short glass. Wet the rim with lime juice and put the glass upside down in coarse salt, so salt clings to the rim (this step is optional). Combine the ingredients for the Classic Margarita in a blender with very ripe fruit (6 to 7 ounces [170 to 200 g] fresh or 4 ounces [115 g] frozen). Add 3/4 cup ice. Blend until smooth and pour into the glass.

TEQUILA SUNRISE

Fill a tall glass with ice. Add:

- 1 ½ ounces (45 ml) silver tequila
- Orange juice almost to fill

Slowly pour ½ ounce (15 ml) grenadine syrup over the top. (As it trickles down it creates the "sunrise" effect.)

Liqueurs, Schnapps, Anise, and Bitters

LIQUEURS, schnapps, anise, and bitters are terms that cover a wide variety of types of spirits. What they all share in common is that they are flavored spirits.

Liqueurs

Also known as cordials, liqueurs are sweet, flavor-infused spirits that are categorized according to the flavoring agent (fruits, nuts, herbal and spice blends, creams, and such). The word *liqueur* comes from the Latin liqui-facere ("to dissolve") and refers to the dissolving of flavorings in the spirits. Artificial flavorings are strictly regulated in most countries, and where allowed they must be prominently labeled as such.

Master distiller **Ted Huber** *pours at* **Huber Starlight Distillery**.

Blended Families

All liqueurs are blends, even those with a primary flavor. A touch of vanilla is added to crème de cacao to emphasize the chocolate. Citrus flavor notes sharpen the presentation of anise. Herbal liqueurs may contain dozens of different flavor elements that a master blender manipulates to achieve the desired flavor profile.

Top-quality liqueurs are produced by distillation of either the fermented flavor materials or the spirit in which they have been infused. Many liqueurs use fin-

Label for **Coffee Liqueur** *by* **McMenamins Edgefield Distillery**

ished spirits such as cognac, rum, or whiskey as their base. Others macerate fruit or other flavorings in a neutral spirit. Crèmes (crème de menthe, crème de cacao, etc.) are liqueurs with a primary flavor, while cream liqueurs combine dairy cream and alcohol in a homogenized, shelf-stable blend.

Liqueurs are not usually aged for any great length of time, but they may undergo resting stages during their production to allow the various flavors to "marry" into a harmonious blend.

Liqueurs can be hard to classify, but regardless of flavor they can be broadly divided into two categories. Generics are liqueurs of a particular type (crème de cacao or curaçao, for example)

A. van Wees De Ooievaar *fruit liqueur from the Netherlands*

Rosolis Ziolowy Gorzki *(stomach bitters) from the* **Lancut Distillery** *in Poland*

Pernod) is produced by distilling anise and a variety of other botanicals together. Pastis is macerated, rather than distilled, and contains fewer botanicals than anis. In Italy, sambuca is distilled from anise and botanicals, but it is then heavily sweetened to make it a liqueur. Oil of fennel (also known as green anise) is frequently added to boost the aroma of the spirit. Greece has a drier, grappa-like liqueur called ouzo, which is stylistically close to pastis.

hat can be made by any producer. Proprietaries are liqueurs with trademarked names that are made according to a specific formula. Examples of such liqueurs include Kahlúa, Grand Marnier, and Southern Comfort.

SCHNAPPS

Schnapps is a general term used for an assortment of white and flavored spirits that have originated in northern countries or regions, such as Germany or Scandinavia. Schnapps can be made from grain, potatoes, or molasses and be flavored with virtually anything (watermelon and root beer schnapps from the United States being proof of that). The dividing line between schnapps and flavored vodka is vague and is more cultural than stylistic.

ANISE-FLAVORED SPIRITS

These spirits can vary widely in style depending on the country of origin. They can be dry or very sweet, low or high proof, distilled from fermented aniseed or macerated in neutral spirit. In France, anis (as produced by

*Tangerine Cello and **Spicy Ginger** organic liqueurs from **New Deal Distillery***

BITTERS

The modern-day descendents of medieval medical potions, bitters are marketed as having at least some vaguely therapeutic value (stomach settlers, hangover cures, and so on). They tend to be flavored with herbs, roots, and botanicals and contain lower quantities of fruit and sugar than liqueurs.

Although there are specialty liqueur producers, most brands are produced by general ditillers as part of an extended product line. Among the new generation of craft distillers, some of the standout liqueur producers include Leopold Brothers Distillery of Denver, Colorado, with their unique whiskey-based fruit liqueurs (the Rocky Mountain Blackberry is particularly noteworthy), and the Flag Hill Distillery in Lee, New Hampshire, with their delicately tinged Sugar Maple Liqueur.

< Label for **Johnny Ziegler Black Forest Style Apple Aux Pomme Schnaps Eau de Vie** by **Winegarden Estate** in New Brunswick, Canada

> Label for **Blackberry Liqueur** by **Clear Creek Distillery**

ABSINTHE MAKES THE HEART GROW FONDER

Modern pastis is the genteel descendent of its much more raffish nineteenth-century ancestor absinthe, a high (sometimes very high) proof anise liquor (technically not a liqueur because no sugar is added) that included extract of wormwood in its list of botanicals. Wormwood contains the chemical compound thujone, whose alleged psychedelic effects made absinthe very popular among the "Bohemian" counter-culture artists and intellectuals of France and Europe (Vincent van Gogh and Oscar Wilde were devotees of what was termed "The Green Fairy"). Conversely, social conservatives and prohibitionists campaigned against it as the crack cocaine of the day and eventually got it outlawed in most European countries and the United States. Modern scientific analysis has found thujone's

Absinthe Verte by **St. George Spirits**

Le Tourment Vert, French Absinthe by Bruno Delannoy of Distillerie Vinet Ege

psychedelic potency to be, at best, greatly exaggerated.

Forbidden fruit is always appealing, and starting in the 1990s absinthe, which continued to be commercially produced in Eastern Europe, slowly started to return to the general marketplace, initially in "thujone-free" versions from France and Switzerland, and more recently from an increasing number of American craft distillers such as North Shore Distilling in Lake Bluff, Illinois, and St. George Distilling in Alameda, California. One thing that has not changed about absinthe is its high alcohol content.

Absinthe Verte by **Leopold Bros.**

PHIL PRICHARD

Prichard's Distillery, Kelso, Tennessee

PHIL PRICHARD was still working in telecom sales in Memphis when he read the classic *The Lore of Still Building* and started teaching himself to make rum.

His first sale came in March of 2001 (thirty cases for $2,929). It was the product of four years of work. His initial plan was to make a product from Tennessee sorghum, but he learned that rum had to come from sugarcane. He wasn't discouraged: "The transition was rather easy. By that time, I had researched the history of American rum, and we just slid into the new profile. It fit very well." Soon, tractor-trailer loads of molasses were being driven in. What sets Prichard's apart from other rum is the use of first-grade sweet molasses, rather than blackstrap. Using better molasses "focused our attention on the production of a traditional American rum," said Prichard. Blackstrap, as well as being used to make rum, is put on cattle and horse feed, and Prichard said: "In Africa they put it on the roads to keep the dust down! It's 32 percent sugar and 68 percent Lord knows what."

Ed Hamilton—noted scholar, author, and keeper of Ministryof Rum.com—said: "By using a high-grade molasses as the raw material, he reduces the need to distill to a high proof in order to reduce the sulfur compounds that are the distiller's bane." The results are evident. "Phil has managed to do what most molasses distillers only wish they could do," said Hamilton, "distill a good white rum and make it drinkable without aging it. Phil makes an impressively smooth white rum that hasn't been aged yet retains the coconut and butterscotch flavors that are its signature."

Prichard takes some of this white rum and barrels it. While the rest of the industry saves money aging their product in used, fifty-two-gallon whiskey barrels, Prichard ages his rum in new, small barrels of fifteen gallons. This provides more surface area for the spirit to interact with the charred oak, and it develops serious flavors not typically found in a rum aged for just three years. Hamilton had more praise: "Prichard's Fine Rum is another great example of the small distiller's art. The relatively low distillation proof and high barrel surface area to volume yield a rum that reminds the imbiber of the other spirits for which Tennessee is more well known."

Prichard is expanding. He bought bourbon from Heaven Hill in Kentucky, aged it again in new barrels, and bottled it as Double Barrel Bourbon. Finishing bourbon this way is rare, (Beam and Buffalo Trace have both experimented with it) and Double Barrel Bourbon was well received. Building a distillery "was difficult beyond imagination. Building a nationwide distribution network has been our greatest challenge and the most costly!" Regardless of the challenges, Prichard moves ever forward: In March of 2009, the distillery began producing its own whiskey.

CHAPTER EIGHT

"Drinking young whiskey is something that is done only in stillhouses and bars in Italy. Let your spirit mature to a proper degree of ripeness."

– Michael Jackson, critiquing an early example of craft distilled whiskey

A GALLERY OF ARTISAN DISTILLERS

*When Iowa flooded, **Jeff Quint** of the **Cedar Ridge Distillery**, filled his still with water to keep it from floating away in the deluge.*

THERE is a spirit revolution happening in the United States, one that will change the entire spirit industry. Distillers with an intense passion for the craft lay their hearts, souls, and economic futures on the line for the purpose of making the ideal liquid spirit. These small companies, sometimes run by one or two people, create a variety of spirits too numerous to mention in a single breath. Their creations and blends are no less valuable or quality-driven than big name brands, some even more so. These niche spirits have the advantage of creativity that expands the scope of what the liquor industry has to offer not only to the U.S., but to the world. These micro-distillers lack the name recognition and the funding that big name companies use to help market their products, but some of them will become the household names of the future—just as Jack Daniels and Johnny Walker, distillers from the past, have become in our time.

- Adapted from Cheri Loughlin's Intoxicologist blog, www.intoxicologist. wordpress.com

The copper patina on the still reflects a variety of colors

THE LEADERS OF THE PACK

ST. GEORGE SPIRITS/HANGAR ONE
ALAMEDA, CALIFORNIA

Each one of the four Holstein stills at Hangar 1 has a different purpose. The still on the right, which is being serviced here, is dedicated to the production of absinthe, the first legal absinthe produced in the United States since 1915. The facility is located in an airplane hangar on the former U.S. Naval Air Station in Alameda, California. Below, the self-proclaimed "Godfather of American artisan distillation," **Jorg Rupf** (left), and **Lance Winters**, the "evil genius" behind **St. George Spirits/Hangar One Vodka**, stand by a state-of-the-art Holstein still, on which Winters can distill brandy, whiskey, absinthe, and vodka.

ANCHOR DISTILLING

Fritz Maytag's stills at **Anchor Distilling** are unique in that the heads can be interchanged depending on what spirit is being distilled. Maytag has brought back historical recipes and classic ways of making spirits.

Spotlight on California Distillers

Stillwater Spirits
PETALUMA, CALIFORNIA

THE SPIRITS of California are as varied as the state. From the blue agave spirit produced by J.B. Wagoner on the southern end of the state to the brandy distilleries scattered through the wine regions, to many fine vodkas, gins, and whiskeys that come out of the San Francisco Bay Area, California is home to many of the pioneers of the artisan distilling movement.

Don Payne flushes the still at **Stillwater Spirits** by pushing a hose through a port window into the column of his Veudome still.

Domaine Charbay
ST. HELENA, CALIFORNIA

Marko Karadesevic stands atop a French Chalvignac Prulho brandy still at **Domaine Charbay**.

SKYROCKET DISTILLERS

Sticking above the blue agave is the heat exchanger for one of the four pot stills at **Skyrocket Distillers**, located on top of a mountain near Temecula, California.

ESSENTIAL SPIRITS

MOSBY WINERY

After a day of distilling, **Bill Mosby** washes down the pot still at the **Mosby Winery** in Buellton, California.

The Moor's head provides a rectifying surface for a unique flavor for the grappa, rum, and other spirits that **Dave Classick** makes in his alambic pot still at **Essential Spirits**.

GERMAIN-ROBIN

Germain-Robin is one of the pioneers of the American craft spirits industry. Its X.O. brandy is considered one of the best brandies in the world. The still is a French Chalvignac Prulho.

Joe Thomas Corley, head distiller at **Germain-Robin**, stands among the experimental racks containing 2.5- and 59-gallon barrels of different types of oak for experimenting with aging brandy.

Sauvignon blanc vines planted in the 1950s grow next to the distillery at **Germain-Robin**.

JEPSON VINEYARDS

A bucket for collecting samples of the wash sits on a spigot at **Jepson Vineyards**.

A **Chalvignac Prulho** brandy still at **Jepson Vineyards**, one of the premier brandy producers in California

OSOCALIS DISTILLERY
SOQUEL, CALIFORNIA

One of the few farm distilleries in California, **Osocalis Distillery** is located deep in the Redwoods in the Santa Cruz Mountains.

Daniel Farber, one of the leading experts on aged brandy in the United States, noses his alambic brandy.

DISTILLING IN TEXAS

GARRISON BROTHERS DISTILLERY

TEXAS

Garrison Brothers Distillery is located in the Texas Hill country, 5.5 miles (88 km) west of Austin, and it is the first legal bourbon distillery in the state. Not shown in this photo, but implied behind the scenes, is the cooking (maturation) of 325 barrels of whiskey, all under the hot Texas sun. **Dennis Todd**, the assistant distiller, is standing in front of the distillery, above.

Distilling in the Pacific Northwest

Clear Creek Distillery
PORTLAND, OREGON

IN THE 1970s, Oregon wineries started producing some the of the best Pinot Noir in the world. The "good beer" movement took over in the late 1980s, and now Portland has found itself at the hub of the new spirits revolution. It is the only city in America that can boast a "Distillery Row," seven distilleries within staggering distance of each other. This proximity has created a keener awareness of quality and a wider variety of unique spirits being produced than anywhere else in the country. Every August, Portland sponsors the Great American Distillers Festival.

Even outside Portland, Oregon is ahead of the curve in the spirits revolution. The state's many distilleries produce organic spirits and many fruit- and honey-based spirits. Many of its fine brandies have yet to reach market and are sitting in barrels waiting to come of age.

Steve McCarthy stands in front of four Holstein stills at the **Clear Creek Distillery** in Portland, Oregon. One of the true pioneers in spirits, McCarthy produces more than thirty-two different spirits ranging from Pear-in-the-Bottle brandy to single malt whiskey.

HIGHBALL DISTILLERY

HOUSE SPIRITS

Michael Klinglesmith, founder of **Highball Distillery**. The Highball Distillery produces Elemental Vodka, a premium organic vodka that launched in June 2008 and is already distributed in three states.

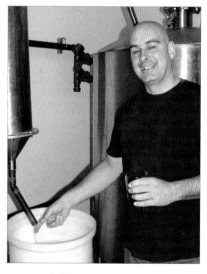

Lee Medoff takes a sample of spirit from the still at **House Spirits Distillery.**

ARTISAN SPIRITS

Ryan Csanky (right) and **Erik Martin**, of **Artisan Spirits**, which makes Apia Artisan Vodka and Martin Ryan Handmade Vodka, lay atop their wine "bladder," which holds 6,000 gallons of Columbia Valley Syrah to be distilled.

The alambic still at **House Spirits Distillery**, whose products include an apothecary line of one-of-a-kind liqueurs available only at the distillery.

INTEGRITY SPIRITS
PORTLAND, OREGON

Rich Philips of **Integrity Spirits** in Portland, Oregon, standing in front of his still.

ROGUE DISTILLERY
PORTLAND, OREGON

Neon sign at the **Rogue Distillery & Public House**

Kieran Sienkiewicz takes a sample of rum from the barrels of the **Rogue Distillery**, whose products include Spruce gin, vodka, dark and white rums, and Hazelnut Spice Rum.

CASCADE PEAK SPIRITS

David Eliason and **Diane Paulson** stand behind the Oregon products at the Great American Distillers Festival, held each fall in Portland, Oregon.

Brandy Peak Distillers

Brandy Peak Distilleries is the only distillery in the United States that heats its still with a wood fire. Their Aged Pear Brandy personifies what a pear eau de vie ought to be and recently won the only double-gold medal awarded at the American Distilling Institutes 2009 judging of brandy, grappa, and eau de vie.

Stringer Orchard Wild Plum Winery

NEW PINE CREEK, OREGON

Wild plums ferment in a stainless steel tank.

DRY FLY DISTILLING

When the new still arrived, **Dry Fly Distilling** had to cut a hole in the ceiling to make room for the column. Their wheat-based vodka won double gold and best vodka at the 2009 San Francisco International Wine and Spirits competition.

Dry Fly has also been very active in getting the laws changed in the state of Washington to allow for the first time tasting rooms at distilleries. A future generation of Washington distillers will benefit from their efforts.

Dry Fly Distilling runs a manual four-head bottle filler. Every spirit is truly hand-crafted.

Left: Painted trout swim in front of a fermentation tank at **Dry Fly Distilling**. Above: **Kent Fleishman** and **Don Poffenroth** are co-owners of Dry Fly.

Idaho Spotlight

IDAHO has a lot more going for it than just spuds, trout, and survivalist camps. In the past decade it has developed a thriving and varied craft distilling culture that includes both the full range of brandy, grain spirits and even rum, but also the U.S.'s first chain of distillery restaurants, modeled on the brewpub concept.

BARDENAY
BOISE, IDAHO

Kevin Settles now runs three distillery/restaurants in Idaho. Sitting on his patio and drinking a hand-crafted "mixology" is something you will talk about for a long time.

KOENIG DISTILLERY AND WINERY
CALDWELL, IDAHO

Andrew Koenig of **Koenig Distillery and Winery** in Caldwell, Idaho.

Colorado Roundup

COLORADO is not far behind the Pacific Northwest in the number of craft distillers. But what it lacks in quantity, it does not lack in quality. There are superlative whiskeys, vodkas, and fruit spirits coming out of Colorado from a unique and varied group of distilleries. Any trip across the distilled spirits map would not be complete without a stop in Colorado.

COLORADO PURE DISTILLING

LAKEWOOD, COLORADO

Rob Masters finishes Colorado Pure Vodka in a glass still and filters it in a custom made charcoal system. This ensures purity of the spirit.

LEOPOLD BROS.

DENVER, COLORADO

For an artisan distillery, Leopold Bros. does it all and does it well. They produce small-batch gin and vodkas, absinthe, Pisco-style brandy, and blackberry-, peach-, and apple-flavored whiskies, along with Three Pins Alpine Herbal Liqueur, New England Cranberry Liqueur, and New York Sour Apple Liqueur.

STRANAHAN'S COLORADO WHISKEY

DENVER, COLORADO

PEACH STREET DISTILLERS

PALISADE, COLORADO

Located in southwest Colorado, a region that is loaded with fruit trees and wineries, **Peach Street Distillers** made its name with pear, peach, and plum brandies and expanded into vodka and gin. They are the first craft distillery to make a bourbon from scratch. And though bourbon may be their best known product, their fruit spirits took five medals at the American Distilling Institute's 2009 judging of brandies, grappas, and eau de vies.

Jess Graber (right) and **Jake Norris** (left) of **Stranahan's Colorado Whiskey**. It all started when volunteer firefighter Jess Graber responded to a fire at whiskey connoisseur George Stranahan's barn. Not only was a long and beautiful friendship formed, so was one of the smoothest and most flavorful whiskeys on a Vendome still.

WYOMING

WYOMING WHISKEY

KIRBY, WYOMING

Steve McNally holds up an artist's rendition of what **Wyoming Whiskey** will be. They represent the big dreams and rapidly changing faces of the craft distilling revolution. The company plans to use about 12,000 bushels of corn and other grains to make 1,000 barrels of whiskey a year. The goal is to produce value-added Wyoming products that agricultural producers can be proud of.

MIDWEST

MANY of the early craft distillers in the U.S. Midwest had their roots in the craft brewing and small-scale winery industries, with a particularly strong contingent of fruit wineries adding on pot stills and producing a wide variety of brandies. But recently a number of new, decidedly urban distilleries have begun operation. Their initial offerings have been gins, vodkas, and the odd absinthe. But the first whiskies are quietly sleeping in their barrels, and waiting for their time to come.

HUBER STARLIGHT DISTILLERY

BORDEN, INDIANA

Huber's Orchard and Winery is second only to the Indianapolis Motor Speedway for top tourist destination in Indiana. Around 650,000 visitors a year enjoy the farmers market, bakery, children's farm park, gift shop, bakery, ice cream factory, cheese shop, Plantation Hall, and distillery. **Ted Huber** was instrumental in getting Indiana laws changed to allow his distillery and is now being followed as more distillers pop up in the state. He is one of the few people to truly wear the title master distiller.

Top: Spring comes to the Huber family farm in rural Indiana, which has been in the family since the mid nineteenth century. Bottom: Ted Huber "noses" a spirit before making a heart cut.

Corn gives **45th Parallel Vodka** its unique flavor profile. This is a story of efficiency and flavor. Soon **45th Parallel Spirits** will be bottling brandy and whiskey as well.

45TH PARALLEL SPIRITS

NEW RICHMOND, WISCONSIN

Built from the ground up, **45th Parallel Spirits** is a blueprint for how craft distillers should handle materials, from corn in to bottled vodka out. 45th Parallel runs a slow distillation process to preserve flavor. Their vodka is triple distilled to achieve purity. Different amounts of carbon filtration are applied to each small batch for flavor consistency.

UNCLE JOHN'S FRUIT HOUSE AND WINERY

ST. JOHNS, MICHIGAN

Uncle John's Fruit House and Winery is located on an apple farm in the center of Michigan. This farm provides a farm/nature experience for families complete with hay rides, corn field mazes, a fling-fruit giant slingshot, a titanic bouncy, playhouses, sandboxes, nature trails, pumpkin patches, train rides through the cherry orchards, wagon rides, duck races, and world-class apple spirits for the ground-ups.

Mike Beck displays the awards that his spirits have received. His products include fortified wines, brandy, and eau-de-vie.

GRAND TRAVERSE DISTILLERY

TRAVERSE CITY, MICHIGAN

Grand Traverse Distillery's rye vodka has won numerous awards, and they now have rye whiskey on the horizon. Watch out, Kentucky: these guys are on the move to change how rye whiskey is perceived. The round barn at right was originally located in Rochester, Indiana. The structure was dismantled, shipped to the northern tip of Michigan, and reassembled. The tasting room inside offers samples of cordials, from apricot to black currant, elderberry to walnut, plus brandy and grappa.

NEW HOLLAND BREWING CO.

HOLLAND, MICHIGAN

New Holland Brewing Co. produces lemon-, orange-, pepper-, raspberry-, vanilla-, and juniper-infused brandies. New Holland's still is hand-crafted from an old navy soup kettle. You can only do this if you own a microbrewery and understand time, temperature, and the flow of ingredients; this is something you can't do at home.

BLACK STAR FARMS

SUTTON BAY, MICHIGAN

Because federal law prohibits a distillery from being located in a house (or in this case a bed-and-breakfast), **Black Star Farms** has a special outbuilding for theirs. One of the purposes of the American Distilling Institute is to change these laws.

Artisan Distillers of the Northeast

CRAFT distillers in the Northeast tend to take their base fermentables very seriously. Potatoes for vodka? Of course. Wheat only? Absolutely. But let's not forget maple syrup. And then there is the matter of what goes into your whiskey...

A double rainbow appears over the buildings at **Vermont Spirits**.

Vermont Spirits makes premium vodkas using local natural ingredients. Their gold vodka is distilled from 100 percent locally farmed maple sap, and their white vodka is distilled from lactose, or milk sugar, producing one of the more unique products on the market. As their slogan says, "You'll never look at a cow the same way again." Vermont Spirits donates a share of their proceeds to charitable causes, including alcohol eduction and alleviating rural poverty worldwide. Above: **Duncan Holaday** (left) and **Steve Johnson** (right) stand next to their custom-made maple sap evaporator. The sap is fermented and later distilled.

SWEETGRASS FARM WINERY AND DISTILLERY

UNION, MAINE

A Hoga pot still at **Sweetgrass Farm Winery and Distillery**.

Adirondack chairs look out over the Upper Medomak Valley.

FLAG HILL WINERY AND DISTILLERY

Graham Hamblett (left) and **Frank Reinhold** (right) of **Flag Hill Winery and Distillery**, whose products include General John Stark Vodka, Sugar Maple Liqueur, and Cranberry Liqueur. Their wine and spirits are sold in eighty-seven liquor stores in New Hampshire, and their spirits are distributed throughout New England.

TRIPLE EIGHT DISTILLERY
NANTUCKET, MASSACHUSETTS

Jay Harman's Triple Eight Distillery, with the help of **Cisco Brewers** and **Nantucket Vineyards**, produces vodka, rum, gin, and "Notch" (Not Scotch) Single Malt Whiskey. For spirits lovers, this is the center of the universe. The Nantucket Chamber of Commerce's weekly meetings are held at the **Cisco Brewery** during the summer months.

These bourbon barrels from Kentucky are for aging spirits. They are filled with rum or whiskey. Triple Eight ages their Hurricane Rum for six months. Their "Notch" (Not Scotch) single malt whiskey ages for five years.

NEWPORT DISTILLING

Newport Distilling makes Thomas Tew Rum from an industrial park in Newport, Rhode Island. Half the building is shared with their brewery. Above is a master brewer and distiller Brett Ryan.

MAINE DISTILLERIES

WESTFORD HILL DISTILLERS

Westford Hill Distillers' eau de vies are revered by their other distillers and take home medals in almost every competition where they are entered. Their Pear eau de vie took gold at the American Distilling Institute's 2009 judging of brandy, grappa, and eau de vie. It was featured in *Saveur* magazine as one of the best one hundred products in the United States.

As with many of the New England distilleries, the **Maine Distilleries** story starts with a heritage of family farming, love of open space, and preservation of land. Local sourcing, clean water, and excellent distillation separate their Cold River Vodka from the competition.

It has garnered double-gold from the 2008 San Francisco Wine and Spirits Competition. *Spirit Journal* gave it five stars and highest recommendation, and *Wine Enthusiast* named it the top vodka in the world in 2008

Chris Dowe is one of the avant-garde in craft distilling. His Cold River Vodka is made exclusively from Maine potatoes on a 1,000-liter Christian Carl pot still.

Maine's first winery/distillery is located deep in the woods at the end of a mile-long dirt road off Route 1 near Gouldsboro, a very long 48 miles (77 km) from Bangor. Winemaker and distiller **Robert Barlett**, above, produces pear, peach, and honey eau de vies, aged apple brandy, and fruit liqueurs.

TUTHILLTOWN SPIRITS

Tuthilltown Spirits sources the grain for their whiskeys from local Hudson Valley producers. Tuthilltown's Baby Bourbon is produced from 100 percent New York corn. They make Heart of the Hudson and Spirit of the Hudson vodkas using fresh cider from nearby orchards. They also make rum, eau de vie, and brandy. **Ralph Erenzo** (right), one of the founding partners, worked with New York State legislators to get the Farm Distillery Act passed, allowing farmers to produce and sell agricultural spirits from their farms. Located at the Tuthilltown Gristmill, a 220-year-old property on the national Registry of Historic Places, their still is located in an old granary.

Exterior shot of **Tuthilltown Spirits**

DISTILLING IN THE CITY OF BROTHERLY LOVE

PHILADELPHIA DISTILLING

The organic juniper berries used to make Bluecoat American Dry gin give a spicy and earthy flavor profile, when compared with London dry gins. The citrus zest and all other botanicals used are also organic. Their hand-hammered, custom-made, gooseneck still is one of a kind. Bluecoat's small batch processing is slow-heated over a ten-hour distillation process. Philadelphia Distilling also produces Penn 1681 Vodka and Vieux Carré Absinthe Superior.

Philadelphia Distilling was the first craft distillery in the State of Pennsylvania. Bluecoat American Dry Gin owns the state and was named best gin at the 2009 San Francisco international Wine and Spirits Competition.

A gooseneck still is used to produce Bluecoat Gin.

RUM, SOUTHERN STYLE

PRICHARDS' DISTILLERY
KELSO, TENNESSEE

SINCE Prohibition, rum has commonly been associated with Caribbean islands, but it was also distilled by famous non-Caribbeans such as George Washington. Mainland rum funded the colonies, the slave trade, and the American Revolution. After Prohibition, it has taken a spirits revolution to bring quality rum back to the forty-eight contiguous states. The South is a natural home to the production of some of the finest rum in the New World, and for that matter, the whole world.

Phil Prichard uses high quality molasses for the production of his award-winning rums. He disdains the use of the traditional black-strap molasses, which he sees as an inferior beginning that produces an inferior distilled spirit. And the proof is in the drink. The more exposure Prichard's Rum achieves, the more accolades it receives. Also, Prichard's Sweet Lucy, a bourbon-based liqueur with apricot and orange, is becoming a campfire favorite, and his Double Barreled Bourbon is winning awards and losing no friends. Prichard has been touting rye whiskey as the true American spirit, and we are all waiting for his entry into this category.

A vendome still produces award-winning rums, whiskies, and other spirits at **Prichards' Distillery.**

CELEBRATION DISTILLATION

Celebration Distillation makes Old New Orleans Rum on a former perfume still that with slight modification became a rum still. Where else but in New Orleans's 9th Ward would a consortium of musicians and artists found a distillery? And why would they distill anything but the local product, sugar cane? Their temperamental and unique still is difficult to work with but produces a robust flavor. In 2007, The American Distilling Institute awarded their Amber Rum the gold medal for aged rums.

Chris Sule (of Celebration Distillation) adds water to the rum wash to adjust its gravity.

COPPER FOX DISTILLERY
SPERRYVILLE, VIRGINIA

Rick Wasmund (above) operates the mash still at the **Copper Fox Distillery**, which is located at the foot of the Blue Ridge Mountains in Sperryville, Virginia. Wasmund is the only distiller in the United States who malts his own barley by hand-firing the malt house with wood cut from his property. Tasting notes for individual batches of his whiskey can be found on his website (see Directory).

CHAPTER NINE

DISTILLING RESOURCES

BEFORE you are going to walk the walk, you first need to learn the talk. The Distiller's Library is a bibliography of just about every English-language book on distilling and the various types of spirits. If you haven't already found what you want in this book, well, here are a whole lot of alternative sources.

The Distiller's Glossary will help you sort out the industry jargon that is sprinkled throughout the text of this book. Learning the meaning of the term *slobber box* alone is worth the price of admission.

And finally, the Directory of Distilleries is simply the most comprehensive worldwide listing of operating whiskey and craft distilleries currently in print. So many tots of whiskey to sample, so little time.

A bartender eyes her pour carefully while serving three Blood on Sand cocktails.

THE DISTILLER'S LIBRARY

Hydrometers for measuring alcohol content of distillates

WHEN it comes to learning about what they make, craft brewers have it relatively easy. Since Michael Jackson's first book on beer came out in the early 1980s, there has been a steady flood of consumer and professional books on beer and brewing arriving on the market. Not so for spirits. The selection is better than it used to be, but the pickings are still slim. Here is a bibliographic summary of what is available.

NOTE: Not all of these books are currently in print, but as of this book's publication, they were all available through Amazon.com or Alibrus.com. The review comments are solely the opinions of the editor, Alan Dikty.

DISTILLED SPIRITS, GENERAL

Blue, Anthony Dias. *The Complete Book of Spirits*. New York: HarperCollins Publishers, 2004.
Wide-ranging review of all major categories of spirits by a well-known beverage and lifestyle writer, with tasting notes and cocktail recopies. Its usefulness is marred by truly awful copyediting.

Dikty, Alan S. *Buying Guide to Spirits*. New York: Sterling Publishing, 1999.
Concise but detailed chapters on all spirits categories, with thousands of tasting notes. Used as a training manual for the sales force of the largest liquor wholesaler in the United States. Written, with a certain dry wit, by the editor of this book.

Henriques, E. Frank. *The Signet Encyclopedia of Whiskey, Brandy & All Other Spirits*. New York: Signet, New American Library, 1979.
CliffsNotes for bar management: quick but informative reference descriptions and explanations for thousands of spirit types, brands, and cocktails. Out of print, but worth searching out.

Lembeck, Harriet. *Grossman's Guide to Wines, Beers, and Spirits*. New York: Charles Scribner's Sons, 1983.
The grand old reference guide to alcoholic beverages: the spirits section is still a good introduction to all the major and many, many of the minor categories and brands.

Owens, Bill, ed. *World Guide to Whiskey Distilleries*. White Mule Press, 2009. www.distilling.com.
A complete listing of whiskey distilleries.

Price, Pamela Vandyke. *A Directory of Wines and Spirits*. London: Peerage Books, 1986.
More wine than spirits oriented, but any reference books that tells the truth about Southern Comfort (it contains no bourbon) is worthwhile.

DISTILLED SPIRITS, HISTORY

Barr, Andrew. *Drink: A Social History of America*. New York: Carroll & Graf Publishers, 1999.
Breezy but well-researched history of drinking in the United States, combined with droll put-down of prohibitionists, past and especially present.

Fleming, Alice. *Alcohol: The Delightful Poison*. New York: Laurel-Leaf Library, Dell Publishing, 1975.
Short history of world and American spirits, followed by an extended essay on the physical effects (positive and negative) of alcohol.

Gately, Ian. *Drink: A Cultural History of Alcohol*. New York: Gotham Books, 2009.
Excellent world history of the development of the drinking of alcohol and how its production, including distilling, has influenced various cultures.

Heron, Craig. *Booze: A Distilled History*. Toronto: Between the Lines, 2003.
A history of liquor in Canada, written from a feminist, politically correct (!!) point of view. Lots of informative history, eh?

Lender, Mark Edward, and **James Kirby Martin**. *Drinking in America: A History*. New York: The Free Press, 1982.
Conventional but well-written survey of liquor drinking in the United States, from Colonial times to the present. Heavily illustrated.

Logsdon, Gene. *Good Spirits*.

White River Junction, VT: Chelsea Green, 1999.
A social history of distillation in the United States, and a call for home distillation. The author is a bit of a crank, but writes well.

Rorabaugh, W. J. *The Alcohol Republic: An American Tradition*. New York: Oxford University Press, 1979.
United States, 1790 to 1830, was the high tide of spirits consumption. Everyone drank, there were no excise taxes, all distilleries were small and local, and best of all, no organized temperance movement. Ah, the Good Old Days.

Waxman, Max. *Chasing the White Dog*. Simon & Schuster, 2009.
Tracing the historical roots of moonshine to the back woods of the United States.

DISTILLED SPIRITS, MEDICINAL EFFECTS

Center for Science in the Public Interest. *Chemical Additives in Booze*. Washington, DC: CSPI Books, 1982.
The CSPI is a notorious collection of public scolds, and no friend to distilled spirits. But their chemical analysis of assorted brands of wines, spirits, and beers makes interesting reading. Hint: Stay away from any liqueur with the word crème in the brand name.

Chafetz, Morris E. *Liquor: The Servant of Man*. Boston: Little Brown, 1965.
Don't let drunken fools screw it up for the rest of us, explained in 223 pages.

Ford, Gene. *The Benefits of Moderate Drinking: Alcohol, Health & Society*. San Francisco: Wine Appreciation Guild, 1988.
Listen to your doctor. Wine (and spirits) in moderation is good for you.

DISTILLED SPIRITS, PHILOSOPHY

Allhoff, Fritz, ed. *Whiskey and Philosophy*. John Wiley & Sons, 2009.
Philosophy of consuming and discussion of whiskey.

Amis, Kingsley. *On Drink*. New York: Harcourt Brace Jovanovich, 1972.
One of Britain's great postwar novelists discusses the purpose of drinking in a series of essays where the wit is as dry as his recipe for a martini.

DeVoto, Bernard. *The Hour*. Boston: Houghton Mifflin, 1951.
One of the United States's great literary critics of the twentieth century explains the importance of good whiskey in a civil society, along with the importance of a properly made martini in "the violet twilight of each day—the cocktail hour."

Edmunds, Lowell. *The Silver Bullet*. Westport, CT: Greenwood Press, 1981.
The martini as a mirror of America's soul. Seven messages from the cocktail shaker.

DISTILLED SPIRITS, PRODUCTION

Barleycorn, Michael. *Moonshiner's Manual*. Hayward, CA: White Mule Press, www.distilling.com.
Home distillation for beginners.

Byrn, M. Lafayette. *The Complete Practical Distiller*. Chagrin Falls, OH: Raudins Publishing, 2002.
Reprinting of 1875 distillery operations manual that contains a lot of still useful information for a small-scale pot distiller. Order at www.raudins.com.

M'Harry, Samuel. *Practical Distiller*. Chagrin Falls, OH: Raudins Publishing, 2001.
Reprinting of 1809 (!) American distilling manual. Learn about distilling techniques from the era of the birth of bourbon. Fascinating reading. Order at www.raudins.com.

Goldsmith, David J. *A Practical Handbook on the Distillation of Alcohol from Farm Products*. Amsterdam: Fredonia Books, 2001.
Reprint of 1922 distilling manual first published during National Prohibition. Just remember, folks: don't drink it, because that would be illegal, wink, wink. Order at www.fredoniabooks.com.

Murtaugh, Dr. John E. *The Alcohol Textbook*. Nottingham, UK: Nottingham University Press, 2003.
Commercial-scale ethanol and beverage alcohol production techniques and reference charts. Not for light reading.

Hundreds of bottles of spirits line the walls in the ultimate well-stocked bar.

Nixon, Mike, and **Mike McGaw**. *The Compleat Distiller*. Auckland, NZ: Amphora Society, 2001. Advanced home distilling from New Zealand. Lots of practical information for newbies.

Owens, Bill. *Craft Whiskey Distilling*. Hayward, CA: White Mule Press, 2009. www.distilling.com. Compact summary of the small-scale distilling process. Heavily illustrated.

Rowley, Matthew. *Moonshine*. Lark Books, 2006. How to build a still at home.

Russell, Inge, ed. *Whiskey Technology*. Academic Press, 2003. Handbook of alcoholic beverages.

Smiley, Ian. *Making Pure Corn Whiskey: A Professional Guide for Amateur and Micro Distillers*. Amphora Society, 2003. www .home-distilling.com A crash course in small-scale distilling from New Zealand, the homeland of modern moonshining.

Stone, John. *Making Gin & Vodka*. Vancouver, BC: John Stone, 1997. Advanced home-distilling techniques for white spirits. Order at www.gin-vodka.com.

BRANDY AND EAU DE VIE

Behrendt, Axel, and **Bibiana Behrendt**. *Cognac*. New York: Abbeville Press, 1997. Detailed tasting notes and histories for more than a hundred producers.

Behrendt, Axel, and **Bibiana Behrendt**. *Grappa: A Guide to the Best*. New York: Abbeville Press, 2000. Extensively researched guide to Italian pomace brandy. Detailed tasting notes and producer histories.

Boudin, Ove. *Grappa: Ialy Bottled*. Partille: PianoForte Publishing, 2007.

Coffee table picture book crossed with a surprisingly detailed explanation of how grappa is produced in Italy, and who does it.

Brown, Gordon. *Handbook of Fine Brandies*. New York: Macmillan, 1990. British-oriented guide to the brandies of the world. Odd bar chart product ratings, but still a good general overview of the subject.

Calabrese, Salvatore. *Cognac: A Liquid History*. London: Cassel, 2001. Big type, lots of pretty pictures, but still a useful reference work, with intelligent tasting notes.

Hannum, Hurst, and **Robert S. Blumberg**. *Brandies and Liqueurs of the World*. Garden City, NJ: Doubleday, 1976. Well-written and still useful overview of the brandies of the world.

Herbert, Malcolm. *California Brandy Cuisine*. San Francisco: Wine Appreciation Guild, 1984.

Primarily a cooking and mixed drink recipe book, it also contains historical notes on the California brandy industry prior to the arrival of modern craft distillers.

Neal, Charles. *Armagnac: The Definitive Guide to France's Premier Brandy*. San Francisco: Flame Grape Press, 1998. Exhaustive guide to every commercial distillery in Armagnac, most of which are tiny farm distilleries. The author loves his topic, hates inferior production techniques, and lets you know exactly what he thinks.

Nicholas, Faith. *Cognac*. London: Mitchell Beazley, 2005. Typical flashy-looking Mitchell Beazley beverage book. Quick history, lots of tasting notes on pricey X.O.s.

Page, C. E. *Armagnac: The Spirit of Gascony*. London: Bloomsbury, 1990. Standard, British-centered guide to Armagnac. Tour and tasting notes.

Ray, Cyril. *Cognac*. New York: Stein & Day, 1973. Well-known British wine writer presents a droll history of France's best-known brandy.

GIN

Coates, Geraldine. *Discovering Gin*. London: NewLifeStyle Publishing, 1996. Flashy graphics and History Lite text on the social history of gin.

Dillon, Patrick. *Gin: The Much-Lamented Death of Madam Geneva*. Boston: Justin, Charles, 2003. The story of the eighteenth-century gin craze in England is even stranger than you can imagine.

Emmons, Bob. *The Book of Gins & Vodkas*. Chicago: Open Court, 2000. Quick but comprehensive introduction to the two primary white spirits.

Watney, John. *Mother's Ruin: The Story of Gin*. London: Peter Owen, 1976. The social history of gin in England. Sloe gin explained!

LIQUEUR

Conrad, Barnaby. *Absinthe: History in a Bottle*. San Francisco: Chronicle Books, 1988. The crack cocaine of its time, but in truth, much maligned. A social history of the "Green Fairy."

Walton, Stuart. *The New Guide to Spirits and Liqueurs*. London: Lorenz Books, 2000. Well-organized reference guide to liqueurs and how to mix them.

White, Francesca. *Cheers! A Spirited Guide to Liquors and Liqueurs*. London: Paddington Press, 1977. Capsule explanations of many liqueurs, well known and obscure.

RUM

Arkell, Julie. *Classic Rum*. London: Prion Books, 1999. Quick-moving survey of rums of the world, with an emphasis on the Caribbean.

Ayala, Luis. *The Rum Experience*. Round Rock, TX: Rum Runner Press, 2001. Enthusiastic guide to the rums of the Americas. Highly opinionated.

Barty-King, Hugh, and **Anton Massel**. *Rum: Yesterday and Today*. London: Heinemann, 1983. Serious history of rum in all of its major markets.

Broom, Dave. *Rum*. London: Mitchell Beazley, 2003. More specifically, rums of the Caribbean for Brit drinkers. Lots of pretty pictures.

Coulombe, Charles A. *Rum: The Epic Story of the Drink That Conquered the World*. New York:

Citadel Press, 2004.
The political history of rum from a Catholic perspective. (Really!)

Gelabert, Blanche. *The Spirit of Puerto Rican Rum*. San Juan: Discovery Press, 1992.
Cooking and mixing drinks with Puerto Rican rum.

Hamilton, Edward. *The Complete Guide to Rum*. Chicago: Triumph Press, 1996.
A yacht-cruising tour of the rums of the Caribbean. A great read.

Hamilton, Edward. *Rums of the Eastern Caribbean*. Culebra, PR: Tafia Publishing, 1997.
The Minister of Rum recycles *The Complete Guide to Rum*.

Obe, Capt. James Pack. *Nelson's Blood: The Story of Naval Rum*. Annapolis: Naval Institute Press, 1983.
Rum as a tool of social control in the Royal Navy. So how much is a tot of rum?

Plotkin, Robert. *Caribe Rum: The Original Guide to Caribbean Rum and Drinks*. Tucson: Bar Media, 2001.
Many, many mixed drink recipes, uniformly enthusiastic product reviews, and a very, very annoying page layout featuring a winged heart (don't ask).

TEQUILA

Emmons, Bob. *The Book of Tequila: A Complete Guide*. Chicago: Open Court, 1997.
Truth in advertising. Excellent introduction to the history and production of tequila. Brand list-

*A bottle of **Northern Comfort Massachusetts Liqueur** sits on the counter at **Nashoba Distillery**.*

ings are now somewhat dated, but still very useful.

Martinez Limon, Enrique. *Tequila: The Spirit of Mexico*. New York: Abbeville Press, 2000.
Extensively illustrated consumer guide to the production and brands of tequila.

Sanchez, Alberto Ruy, and **Margarita de Orellana**. *Tequila: A Traditional Art of Mexico*. Washington: Smithsonian Books, 2004.
Breezy, lightweight guide to current brands of tequila. Lots of drink recipes.

Valenzuela-Zapata, Ana G., and **Gary Paul Nabhan**. *Tequila! A Natural and Cultural History*. Tucson: The University of Arizona Press, 2003.
Tequila as seen through the eyes of plant biologists.

VODKA

Begg, Desmond. *The Vodka Companion*. Philadelphia: Running Press, 1998.
Quick history of vodka with extensive tasting notes.

Delos, Gilbert. *Vodkas of the World*. Edison, NJ: Wellfleet Press, 1998.
Excellent survey of vodkas and

aquavit.

Wisniewski, Ian. *Vodka: Discovering, Exploring, Enjoying*. London: Ryland Peters & Small, 2003.
A stylish magazine article on vodka turned into a very short book.

WHISKEY, GENERAL

Gabanyi, Stefan. *WHISK(E)Y*. New York: Abbeville Press, 1997.
English translation of a German guide to the whiskies of the world. Thousands of brands and terms listed and explained. Excellent quick reference guide.

Jackson, Michael. *WHISKEY*. New York: Dorling Kindersley, 2005.
Heavily detailed and beautifully laid-out guide to the whiskies of the world, including the new craft distillers. Required addition to any serious distiller's library.

Jackson, Michael. *The World Guide to Whisky*. Topsfield, MA: Salem House Publishers, 1988.
The Bard of Brew's first take on the whiskies of Scotland, Ireland, Canada, the United States, and Japan. A worthy companion to his seminal *The World Guide to Beer*.

MacLean, Charles. *Whiskey (Eyewitness Companions)*. London: Dorling Kindersley, 2008.
Lightweight but up-to-date listing of all major and a sprinkling of smaller whiskey distilleries worldwide, with limited tasting notes. Heavily illustrated in the patent DK publication style.

The George Washington Distillery

Murphy, Brian. *The World Book of Whiskey*. Chicago: Rand Mc-Nally & Co., 1979.
Interesting view of the whiskies of the world just before the late twentieth-century rash of mergers, closures, and brand changes. Après moi, le deluge.

Murray, Jim. *The Complete Guide to Whiskey*. Chicago: Triumph Books, 1997.
More properly a guide to Scotch, Irish, Canadian, and American whiskies, and the distilleries that make them. Good capsule histories of the distilleries with minimal tasting notes.

Murray, Jim. *Jim Murray's Whiskey Bible: 2006*. London: Carlton Books, 2006.
Close to all-encompassing pocket tasting guide to the world's whiskies from Britain's other leading spirits writer.

WHISKEY, AMERICAN— GENERAL

Getz, Oscar. *Whiskey: An American Pictorial History*. New York: David McKay, 1978.

Excellent pictorial history of liquor and distilling in American society.

Waymack, Mark H., and **James F. Harris**. *The Book of Classic American Whiskeys*. Chicago: Open Court, 1995.
Concise history of American whiskey and current distilleries with detailed tasting notes.

WHISKEY, AMERICAN— BIOGRAPHY

Green, Ben A. *Jack Daniel's Legacy*. Nashville: Rich Printing, 1967.
Quasi-official biography of the founder of America's leading whiskey distillery.

Krass, Peter. *Blood & Whiskey: The Life and Times of Jack Daniel*. Hoboken, NJ: John Wiley & Sons, 2004.
Interesting analysis of the life of Jack Daniel and his business world.

Pacult, F. Paul. *American Still Life: The Jim Beam Story*. Hoboken, NJ: John Wiley & Sons, 2003.
Standard recap of American whiskey distilling history with an emphasis on the growth of the Jim

Bean Distillery and its brands.

Taylor, Richard. *The Great Crossing: A Historic Journey to Buffalo Trace Distillery*. Frankfort, KY: Buffalo Trace Distillery, 2002.
Well-written company history with good insights into the development of bourbon distilling in early Kentucky.

Van Winkle Campbell, Sally. *But Always a Fine Bourbon: Pappy Van Winkle and the Story of Old Fitzgerald*. Louisville: Limestone Lane Press, 1999.
Self-satisfied family history with lots of pretty pictures.

WHISKEY, AMERICAN— BOURBON & TENNESSEE

Carson, Gerald. *The Social History of Bourbon*. Lexington: University Press of Kentucky, 1984.
The evolving role of bourbon in America's collective lifestyle.

Cecil, Sam K. *The Evolution of the Bourbon Whiskey Industry in Kentucky*. Paducah, KY: Turner Publishing, 1999.
County-by-county listings and capsule histories of every distillery to operate in Kentucky. An obvious labor of love.

Cowdery, Charles K. *Bourbon, Straight: The Uncut and Unfiltered Story of American Whiskey*. Chicago: Made and Bottled in Kentucky, 2004.
An independent and frequently irreverent view of the American bourbon industry. Must reading

*An old truck outside **Stranahan's** Colorado Whiskey*

for all serious students of American whiskey distilling.

Crowgey, Henry G. *Kentucky Bourbon: The Early Years of Whiskeymaking*. Lexington: University Press of Kentucky, 2008.
More properly a remarkably detailed history of the development of commercial distilling in Colonial America and the early United States. Substantial original scholarship. Who knew that peach brandy was once produced by most Southern whiskey distillers?

Givens, Ron. *Bourbon at Its Best: The Lore and Allure of America's Finest Spirits*. Cincinnati: Clerisy Press, 2008.
Lavishly illustrated coffee-table book introduction to bourbon.

Murray, Jim. *Classic Bourbon, Tennessee and Rye Whiskey*. London: Prion Books, 1996.
An Englishman tastes American whiskies, and likes them. Extensive tasting notes.

Regan, Gary, and **Mardee Haidin Regan**. *The Book of Bourbon*. Shelburne, VT: Chapters Publishing, 1995.
Extensive tasting notes, somewhat dated at this point, and recipes.

Regan, Gary, and **Mardee Haidin Regan**. *The Bourbon Companion*. Philadelphia: Running Press, 1998.
CliffsNotes for virtually all current brands of bourbon.

WHISKY, CANADIAN

Bingham, Madeleine. *King of the Castle: The Making of a Dynasty: Seagram's and the Bronfman Empire*. New York: Atheneum, 1979.
The dirt on the now vanished dom-inant force in Canadian distilling.

Bronfman, Samuel. *From Little Acorns: The Story of Distillers Corporation-Seagrams, Ltd.* Montreal: Distillers Corporation-Seagrams Limited, 1970.
The Grand Old Man of Canadian Distilling tells a cleaned-up version of the history of Seagrams and Canadian whisky. Nary a mention of Joe Kennedy and bootlegging.

Brown, Lorraine. *200 Years of Tradition: The Story of Canadian Whisky*. Toronto: Fitzhenry & Whiteside, 1994.
A non-Seagramscentric history of Canadian whisky. A bit on the short side.

Marrus, Michael R. *Samuel Bronfman: The Life and Times of Seagram's Mr. Sam*. Boston: University Press of New England, 1991.
Academic analysis of the Canadian distilling industry through an overview of the now dismantled Seagrams whisky empire.

Rannie, William F. *Canadian Whisky: The Product and the Industry*. Lincoln, ON: W. F. Rannie Publisher, 1976.
Interesting snapshot of the Canadian distilling industry on the eve of the late-twentieth-century industry consolidation.

WHISKEY, MOONSHINE—HISTORY

Carr, Jess. *The Second Oldest Profession: An Informal History of Moonshining in America*. Englewood Cliffs, NJ: Prentice-Hall, 1972.
The history of moonshining, primarily in Southern states.

Dabney, Joseph Earl. *Mountain Spirits*. Asheville, NC: Bright Mountain Books, 1974.
A social history of Appalachian moonshine distilling with an attitude. Corn whiskey: good; sugar distillation: bad.

Dabney, Joseph Earl. *More Mountain Spirits*. Asheville, NC: Bright Mountain Books, 1980.
There is more to moonshine than just corn whiskey; peach brandy, for example. Chockfull of recipes and homemade still designs.

Keller, Esther. *Moonshine: Its History and Folklore*. New York: Weathervane Books, 1971.
Moonshine in Kentucky and southern Indiana. Lightweight, but entertaining.

Barrels roll out at **Woodford Reserve Distillery**.

Mauer, David W. *Kentucky Moonshine*. Lexington: University Press of Kentucky, 1974.
Moonshining as an industry, from Colonial times to the present.

WHISKEY, IRISH

Magee, Malachy. *Irish Whiskey: A 1000 Year Tradition*. Dublin: O'Brien Press, 1998.
Short but detailed history of Irish whiskey distilling, with capsule histories of every commercial distillery in Ireland.

McGuffin, John. *In Praise of Poteen*. Belfast: Applegate Press, 1978.
Moonshine, Irish style. As is usually the case, romantic history is better than the rather squalid current state of affairs, with kitchen stills in urban housing estates distilling fermented sugar water.

McGuire, E. B. *Irish Whiskey*. Dublin: Gill & Macmillan, 1973.
A last hurrah view of the Irish distilling industry, just prior to the final industry consolidation.

Murray, Jim. *Classic Irish Whiskey*. London: Prion Books, 1998.
More or less complete tasting and buying guide to Irish whiskey, including local brands. Murray does tend to like everything, though.

Townsend, Brian. *The Lost Distilleries of Ireland*. Glasgow: Neil Wilson, 1999.
Companion book to the author's *Scotch Missed: The Lost Distilleries of Scotland*, only sadder. Scotland still has around a hundred distilleries, while Ireland has only three.

WHISKY, SCOTCH

Barnard, Alfred. *The Whisky Distilleries of the United Kingdom*. Edinburgh: Birlinn, 2003.
Reprint of 1887 guide to the distilleries of Scotland, England, and Ireland. Wonderful window into a long vanished world of distilling, with many engravings. A must-have for the historically minded distiller.

Brander, Michael. *The Essential Guide to Scotch Whisky*. Edinburgh: Canongate Publishing, 1990.
Compact report on the state of the Scottish distilling industry, circa 1990.

Cooper, Derek. *A Taste of Scotch*. London: Andre Deutsch, 1989.
The role of Scotch whisky in various facets of British culture. Lots of great graphics.

Daiches, David. *Scotch Whisky: Its Past and Present*. New York: Macmillan, 1970.
The world of Scotch whisky distill-ing, just prior to the late-twentieth-century shutdowns.

Graham, Duncan, and **Wendy Graham**. *Visiting Distilleries, 2nd edition*. Glasgow: Angel's Share, 2003.
Does your favorite Highland distillery have a gift shop? How clean is the loo? All your Whisky Trail questions are answered here.

Greenwood, Malcolm. *A Nip Around the World: The Diary of a Whisky Salesman*. Argyll: Argyll Publishing, 1995.
Stories from the front of whisky selling in Europe. Interesting, but short.

Gunn, Neil M. *Whisky & Scotland: A Practical and Spiritual Survey*. Edinburgh: Souvenir Press, 1988.
Scotch Malt Whisky Society reprint of 1935 classic tome on Scotch whisky production and history.

*Barrels set for aging tequila in the warehouse/tasting room at the **Casa Cofradia Distillery**, in Tequila, Jalisco, Mexico*

Hume, John R., and **Michael S. Moss**. *The Making of Scotch Whisky, revised edition*. Edinburgh: Canongate, 2000.
A business history of Scottish distilling. Very detailed, yet well written.

Jackson, Michael. *Michael Jackson's Complete Guide to Single Malt Scotch, 5th edition*. Philadelphia: Running Press, 2004.
The benchmark guide to single malt Scotch whiskies, with more than a thousand tasting notes. A must-have reference book.

Jackson, Michael. *Scotland and Its Whiskies*. New York: Harcourt, 2001.
A travel guide to the various distilling regions of Scotland. Lovely photographs and lyrical text from Britain's leading spirits and beer writer.

Lockhart, Sir Robert Bruce. *Scotch: The Whisky of Scotland in Fact and Story*. London: Putnam, 1970.
A standard history of Scotch whisky, much used (quoted and otherwise) by subsequent books on the topic.

MacLean, Charles. *MacLean's Miscellany of Whisky*. London: Little Books, 2004.
A collection of whisky-themed essays on a wide variety of topics. Great bedside book.

MacLean, Charles. *The Mitchell Beazley Pocket Whisky Book*. London: Mitchell Beazley, 1993.
Pocket guide with ratings on single malt, grain, and blended Scotch whiskies. Now somewhat dated.

McDougall, John, and **Gavin D. Smith**. *Wort, Worms & Washbacks: Memoirs from the Stillhouse, Glasgow*: Angel's Share, 2000.
Journeyman still master's tales of life in a variety of Scottish distilleries. Old slights and scores are settled in a most amusing manner.

McDowall, R. J. S. *The Whiskies of Scotland*. New York: Abelard-Schuman, 1967.
Distilleries, blenders, and their whiskies of the time are described in extensive detail, while American mixers are denounced as foul pollutants of pure malt spirits.

Milroy, Wallace. *Wallace Milroy's Malt Whisky Almanac*. New York: St. Martin's Press, 1991.
Limited tasting notes on single malt whiskies from an early British advocate of the style.

Morrice, Philip. *The Schweppes Guide to Scotch*. Sherborne, UK: Alphabooks, 1983.
All-encompassing guide to every Scotch whisky distiller, blender, merchant, bottler, and marketing group. Somewhat outdated now, but still a useful reference guide.

Reeve-Jones, Alan. *A Dram Like This . . .* London: Elm Tree Books, 1974.
Droll social history of Scotch whisky with extensive mixed drink and food recipes.

Townsend, Brian. *Scotch Missed: Scotland's Lost Distilleries*, 3rd edition. Glasgow: Angel's Share, 2004.
The life and death of more than a hundred Scottish distilleries are chronicled with photographs and directions. Try cross-referencing it with Barnard's *The Whisky Distilleries of the United Kingdom*.

The Distiller's Glossary

Agitator: A device such as a stirrer that provides complete mixing and uniform dispersion of all components in a mixture. Agitators are generally used continuously during the cooking process and intermittently during fermentation.

Alcohol: The family name of a group of organic chemical compounds composed of carbon, hydrogen, and oxygen; includes methanol, ethanol, isopropyl alcohol, and others.

Applejack: In its original meaning, fermented hard apple cider that is partially frozen to separate the water from the alcohol. In modern terms, it is the North American version of apple brandy.

Atmospheric pressure: Pressure of the air and atmosphere surrounding us that changes from day to day. It is equal to 14.7 psi.

Auger: A rotating, screw-type device that moves material through a cylinder. In alcohol production, it is used to transfer grains from storage to the grinding site to the cooker.

Baker's yeast: Standard robust yeast used openly by bakers, and quietly by many distillers. The fermentation is quick and violent, and the resulting beer is cloudy. But that really doesn't matter if you are going to distill it.

Balling: On a hydrometer, the measurement of the percent of sugar in a solution by weight. See Brix.

Barrel: Varies depending on country. In U.S. terms, a liquid measure equal to 42 American gallons or about 306 pounds; one barrel equals 5.6 cubic feet or 0.159 cubic meters.

Batch distillation: A process in which the liquid feed is placed in a single container and the entire volume is heated, in contrast to continuous distillation, in which the liquid is fed continuously through the still.

Batch fermentation: Fermentation conducted from start to finish in a single vessel.

Batch process: Unit operation where one cycle of feed stock preparation, cooking, fermentation, and distillation is completed before the next cycle is started.

BATF: Formerly the Bureau of Alcohol, Tobacco, and Firearms; under the U.S. Department of Treasury. Responsible for the issuance of permits, both experimental and commercial, for the production of alcohol. The guns have been removed and the agency has been renamed the Tobacco and Taxation Bureau (TTB).

Beer: A general term for all fermented malt beverages flavored with hops. A low-level (6 to 12 percent) alcohol solution derived from the fermentation of mash by microorganisms. For distillers, the initial fermented grain solution that is distilled. See Wash.

Beer still: The stripping section of a distillation column for concentrating ethanol.

Boiler: A unit base to heat water to produce steam for cooking and distillation processes.

Bourbon: Whiskey produced within the United States from a mash containing a minimum of 51 percent corn and then aged for a minimum of two years in a new charred oak barrel. Bourbon can be legally produced in any state.

Brandy: Generally speaking, the result of distilling any fermented fruit wine. Specifically, the result of distilling grape wine. Fruit brandies are made from fruits other than grapes, while fruit-flavored brandies are usually grape brandy with added fruit flavors. See Eau de vie and Grappa.

Brewing: Generically, the entire beer-making process, but technically only the part of the process during which the beer wort is cooked in a brew kettle and during which time the hops are added. After brewing, the beer is fermented. In a grain distillery, the fermented wort or wash is frequently referred to as *beer*.

Brix: A measurement of sweetness in a liquid, usually fruit juice. Specifically the measurement of dissolved sugar-to-liquid mass ratio of a liquid. As an example, in a 100-gram solution, a 30 Brix measurement is 30 grams of sugar and 70 grams of liquid.

Bubble-cap trays: Cross-flow trays usually installed in rectifying columns handling liquids free of suspended solids. The bubble caps consist of circular cups inverted over small vapor pipes. The vapor from the tray below passes

Detail of a toasted barrel

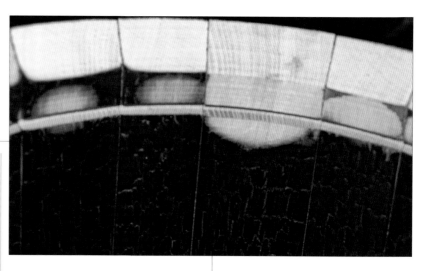

through the vapor pipes into the caps and curves downward to escape below the rim into the liquid. The rim of each cap is slotted or serrated to break up the escaping vapor into small bubbles, thereby increasing the surface area of the vapor as it passes through the liquid.

Cachaca: Unaged, raw sugarcane spirit from Brazil, usually mixed with neutral grain spirit from other sources.

Cane spirit: The broad term for spirits distilled from fermented sugarcane juice. See Cachaca and Rum.

Cognac: By legal-definition, grape brandy from the Cognac region of France.

Column: A vertical, cylindrical vessel used to increase the degree of separation of liquid mixtures by distillation or extraction.

Compound: A chemical term denoting a combination of two or more distinct elements.

Concentration: The ratio of mass or volume of solute present in a solution to the amount of solvent. The quantity of ethyl alcohol (or sugar) present in a known quantity of water.

Condenser: A heat-transfer device that reduces a thermodynamic fluid from its vapor phase to its liquid phase.

Continuous fermentation: A steady-state fermentation system that operates without interruption; each stage of fermentation occurs in a separate section of the fermenter, and flow rates are set to correspond with required residence times.

Cooker: A tank or vessel designed to cook a liquid or extract or digest solids in suspension; the cooker usually contains a source of heat and is fitted with an agitator.

Cooking: The process that breaks down the starch granules in the grain, making the starch available for the liquefaction and saccharification steps of the fermentation process.

Coproducts: The resulting substances and materials that accompany the production of ethanol by distillation.

Corn whiskey (likker): Legally: Minimum 80 percent corn mash whiskey, aged a minimum of two years in used wooden barrels. Illegally: The fresh-from-the-still original version of moonshine. See Moonshine.

Cross-flow trays: Liquid flows across the tray and over a weir to a downcomer that carries it to the next lower tray. Vapors rise from the bottom of the column to the top, passing through the tray openings and the pools of cross-flowing liquid.

Denature: The process of adding a substance to ethyl alcohol to make it unfit for human consumption; the denaturing agent may be gasoline or other substances specified by the Bureau of Alcohol, Tobacco, and Firearms.

Dewatering: To remove the free water from a solid substance.

Distillate: That portion of a liquid that is removed as a vapor and condensed during a distillation process.

Distillation: The process of separating the components of a mixture by differences in boiling point; a vapor is formed from the liquid by heating the liquid in a vessel and successively collecting and condensing the vapors into liquids.

Eau de vie: Colorless fruit brandy such as Kirschwasser from the Schwartzwald in Germany.

Ethanol: The alcohol product of fermentation that is used in alcohol beverages and for industrial purposes; chemical formula blended with gasoline to make gasohol; also known as ethyl alcohol or grain alcohol.

Ethyl alcohol: A flammable organic compound formed during sugar fermentation. It is also called ethanol, grain alcohol, or simply alcohol.

Label for **Cherry Liqueur** by *Clear Creek Distillery*

Evaporation: The conversion of a liquid to the vapor state by the addition of latent heat or vaporization.

Fermentation: A microorganically mediated enzymatic transformation of organic substances, especially carbohydrates, generally accompanied by the evolution of a gas. The process in which yeast turns the sugars present on malted grains into alcohol and carbon dioxide.

Gasohol (Gasahol): Registered trade names for a blend of 90 percent unleaded gasoline with 10 percent fermentation ethanol.

Gasoline: A volatile, flammable liquid obtained from petroleum that has a boiling range of approximately 29° to 216°C and is used for fuel for spark ignition internal combustion engines.

Gin: White spirit flavored with juniper berry and other "botanicals."

Grappa: A brandy distilled from grape pomace.

Head: The end (enclosure) of a cylindrical shell. The most commonly used types of heads are hemispherical, ellipsoidal, flanged and dished (semispherical), conical, and flat.

Heads: The initial run of distillate at the start of the distillation process. Heads are usually returned to the still for redistillation.

Heat exchanger: A unit that transfers heat from one liquid (or vapor) to another without mixing the fluids. A condenser is one type of heat exchanger.

Hops: The dried blossom of the female hop plant, which is a climbing herb (*Humulus lupulus*). Aged hops are used by some whiskey distillers in the mashing process.

Lauter tun: The vessel used in brewing between the mash tun and the brew kettle. It separates the barley husks from the clear liquid wort. The barley husks themselves help provide a natural filter bed through which the wort is strained. This filtration is frequently skipped in grain distillation.

Lautering: The process of straining wort in a lauter tun before it is cooled in the brew kettle.

Mash: A mixture, consisting of crushed grains and water, that can be fermented to produce ethyl alcohol.

Mashing: The process by which barley malt is mixed with water and cooked to turn soluble starch into fermentable sugar. Other cereal grains, such as corn and rice, may also be added. After mashing in a mash tun, the mash is filtered through a lauter tun, where upon it becomes known as wort.

Methyl alcohol: A poisonous type of alcohol, also known as wood alcohol. Produced as a by-product of the fermentation of starch or cellulose. Methyl alcohol is not produced by fermenting sugar, and only minimally from fruit wine.

Mezcal: Distilled spirit from the pulp of the agave plant, produced in Mexico outside of the designated tequila production area. See Tequila.

Moonshine: Originally minimally aged corn whiskey produced illegally in the Appalachian Mountain region of the Southern United States. Modern moonshine is usually made from fermented sugar water. See Corn whiskey.

Pot: A hollow vessel more deep than broad.

Pressure vessel: A metal container generally cylindrical or spheroid, capable of withstanding various loadings.

Prohibition: The process by which a government prohibits its citizens from buying or possessing alcoholic beverages. Specifically, Prohibition refers to the period between the effective date of the 18th Amendment to the U.S. Constitution (January 16, 1920) and its repeal by the 21st Amendment. Repeal took effect on December 5, 1933, although it passed Congress in February, and the sale of beer was permitted after April 7, 1933.

Proof: Alcohol containing 50 percent alcohol by volume (ABV) is called 100 U.S. proof spirit. U.S. proof is twice the percentage of spirit by volume.

Rectification: With regard to distillation, the selective increase of the concentration of the lower volatile component in a mixture by successive evaporation and condensation.

Rectifying column: The portion of a distillation column above the feed tray in which rising vapor is enriched by interaction with a

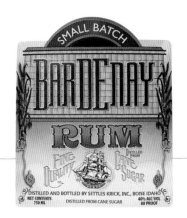
*Label for **Bardenay Rum***

countercurrent falling stream of condensed vapor.

Rum: A distilled spirit made from fermented molasses or sugarcane juice.

Rye whiskey: Whiskey containing a minimum of 51 percent rye grain, aged for at least two years in a new charred oak barrel. Rye whiskey, which was the original whiskey in Colonial America, has a dry, hard-edged palate, and is nowadays primarily blended into other types of whiskey to give them more character.

Shell: Structural element made to enclose some space. Most of the shells are generated by the revolution of a plane curve.

Shower-type trays: These trays do not have downcomers. The liquid level results from the pressure drop caused by the counterflowing streams.

Sieve trays: Sieve trays are usually cross-flow type perforated with small holes. Sieve trays are sometimes used for feeds that tend to deposit solids or polymerize in the column.

Sight gauge: A clear calibrated cylinder through which liquid level can be observed and measured.

Slobber box: Pressure relief and particulate matter filter chamber located between the still and condenser coils on a pot still.

Still: An apparatus for distilling liquids, particularly alcohols; it consists of a vessel in which the liquid is vaporized by heat, and a cooling device in which the vapor is condensed.

Stripping column: The section of the distillation column in which the alcohol concentration in the starting beer solution is decreased. This section is below the beer injection point.

Stripping section: The section of a distillation column below the feed in which the condensate is progressively decreased in the fraction of more volatile component by stripping.

Tails: The final discharge of the distillation process, tails contain undesirable flavor elements (congeners) and fusel oils, and they are usually discarded.

Tank: A vessel of large size to contain liquids.

Tequila: Distilled spirit from the fermented pulp of the agave plant, produced by legal definition only in certain designated areas in and around the Mexican state of Jalisco. See Mezcal.

Tunnel-cap trays: Tunnel-cap trays are similar to bubble-cap trays except that they are rectangular.

Valve trays: Valve trays are cross-flow trays with large perforations that are covered with flat plates. The cover plates are free to move vertically and thus permit the passage of ascending vapors.

Vaporization: The process of converting a compound from a liquid or solid state to the gaseous state. Alcohol is vaporized during the distillation.

Vessel: A container or structural envelope in which material is processed, treated, or stored; for example, pressure vessels, reactor vessels, agitator vessels, and storage vessels (tanks).

Vodka: In U.S. terms, colorless, odorless, tasteless neutral spirit. Foreign vodkas can retain flavor elements, particularly if pot distilled.

Wash: In distilling, the liquid produced by the fermentation process, which is then distilled to concentrate the alcohol. See Beer.

Worm: Copper condenser coils suspended in a vessel of continuously flowing cold water, used as part of a pot still.

Wort: An oatmeallike substance consisting of water and mash barley in which soluble starch has been turned into fermentable sugar during the mashing process. The liquid remaining from a brewing mash preparation following the filtration of fermentable beer. In grain distillation, the wort or mash is frequently fermented and then distilled without filtration.

Yeast: The enzyme-producing one-celled fungi of the genus Saccharomyces that is added to wort before the fermenting process for the purpose of turning fermentable sugar into alcohol and carbon dioxide.

INTERNATIONAL DIRECTORY OF DISTILLERIES

CLEAR CREEK DISTILLERY

Brandy made from organically grown Mirabelle plums from King Estate

Eau de Vie of *Mirabelle*

Distilled & Bottled by Clear Creek Distillery

PORTLAND, OR, U.S.A. • 375 ML. • 40% ALC. BY VOL.

Label for **Mirabell Eau de Vie**

AUSTRALIA

Bakery Hill
28 Ventnor Street
North Balwyn Victoria 3104
www.bakeryhilldistillery.com.au

Great Southern Distilling Company
252 Frenchman Bay Road
Albany
www.distillery.com.au

Hellyers Road
153 Old Surrey Road, PO Box 1415
Burnie, Tasmania 7320
www.hellyersroaddistillery.com.au

Wild Swan Distilling
94 Burniston Street
Scarborough, WA 6019
wildswandistillery.com.au

AUSTRIA

Reisetbauer
A-4062 Axberg 15
Axberg
www.reisetbauer.at

Waldviertler Roggenhof
3664 Roggenreith 3 Martinsberg,
Niederösterreich
Martinsberg, Zwettl
www.roggenhof.at

Weidenauer
Leopolds 6, 3623 Kottes
Leopolds Kottes Purk, Zwettl
www.weidenauer.at

Weutz
St Nikolai 6
8505 St Nikolai im Sausal
www.weutz.at

Wolfram Ortner
Untertscherner Weg 3
9546 Bad Kleinkirchheim,
Spittal an der Drau
www.wob.at

BELGIUM

The Owl Distillery
Rue Sainte Anne 94
Grâce-Hollogne
www.belgianwhisky.com

CANADA

Glenora Inn & Distillery
Route 19/Ceilidh Trail
Glenville, Cape Bretonm Nova
Scotia
glenoradistillery.com

Kittlingridge Spirits
297 South Service Road
Grimsby, ON L3M 1Y6
kittlingridge.com

Okangan Spirits
2920 28th Avenue
Vernon, BC V1T 1V9
okanaganspirits.com

Philips Brewing Co.
2010 Government Street

Victoria, BC V8T 4P1
phillipsbeer.com

Winchester Cellars
6170 Old West Saanich
Victoria, BC V9E 2G8
winchestercellars.com

Winegarden Estate
851 Route 970
Baie Verte, New Brunswick E4M
1Z7
winegardenestate.com

CZECH REPUBLIC

Gold Cock Distillery
Razav 472
763 12 Vizovice
www.rjelinek.cz

DENMARK

Destilleriet Braunstein
Carlsensvej 5 – 4600 Köge
Koge, Sjaelland
www.braunstein.dk

Fary Lochan Destilleri
Co/Smedevej 15, Farre
DK – 7323 Give
www.farylochan.com

Ørbaek Bryggeri
Orbaek Bryggeri Assensvej 38,
5853 Orbaek
Orbaek, Funen (Island)
www.www.oerbaek-bryggeri.nu

Stauning Whisky A/S
6900 Skern
Denmark
stauningwhisky.dk
www.stauningwhisky.dk

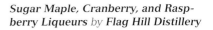
Sugar Maple, Cranberry, and Raspberry Liqueurs by *Flag Hill Distillery*

Vingården Lille Gadegård
v. Jesper Paulsen
Sondre Landevej 63
DK-3720 Aakirkeby
www.a7.dk

ENGLAND

St. George's Distillery
English Whisky Co, Ltd.
Harling Road
Roudham Norfolk NR16 2QW
www.englishwhisk.co.uk

FINLAND

Teerenpeli Malt Whisky Distillery
Hämeenkatu 19, Lahti
www.teerenpeli.com

FRANCE

Des Menhirs
Pont Menhir 29700
Plomelin, Bretagne
www.distillerie.fr

Distillerie Bertrand
3 Rue du Marechal Leclerc – BP 21
350 Uberach, Alsace
www.distillerie-bertrand.com

Domaine Mavela
Route de La Marana – 20600
Furiani
www.brasseriepietra.com

Fisselier
56 Rue de Verger, 35571 Chantepie
www.jacques-fisselier.com

Glann ar Mor
Celtic Whisky Compagnie
Crec'h ar Fur, 22610 Pleubian
Bretagne
www.glannarmor.com

Guillon
Hameau de Vertuelle, 51 150
Louvois
Champagne-Ardenne
www.whisky-guillon.com

Wambrechies
1, Rue de la Distillerie
F- 59118 Wambrechies
www.wambrechies.com

Warenghem
Route de Guingamp, 22300 Lannion, Brittany
www.distillerie-warenghem.com

GERMANY

Berghof Rabel
Berghof 73277 Owen-Teck
Schliengen, Baden-Wurttemberg
www.berghof-rabel.de

Blaue Maus
Bambergerstrasse 2, 91330
Eggolsheim-Neuses
Ebermannstadt, Bavaria
www.fleischmann-whisky.de

Brennerei Höhler
Kirchgasse 3, 65326 Aarbergen,
Hesse
www.brennerei-hoehler.de

Lantenhammer Destillerie
Bayrischzeller Strasse 13, 83727
Schliersee, Bavaria
www.slyrs.de

Reiner Mösslein
Weingut Reiner Mösslein,
Untere Dorfstrasse 8, 97509 Zeilitzheim, Bavaria
www.weingeister.de

Sonnenschein
Alter Fährweg 7-9 – 58456 Witten-Heven
North Rhine-Westphalia
www.sonnenschein-brennerei.de

JAPAN

Fuji-Gotemba
www.kirin.co.jp

Hakushu (and Yamazaki)
Daiba 2-3-3, Minato-ku
Tokyo 135-8631
www.suntory.co.jp

Hanyu
+81 (0)3 5418 4611
www.one-drinks.com

Karuizawa
www.mercian.co.jp

Sendai (Miyagikyo) and Yoichi
5-4-31, Minami-Aoyama, Minato-ku

Tokyo 107-8616
www.nikka.com

INDIA

Amrut Distilleries, Ltd.
41/1, 72nd Cross,
Rajajinagar 6th Block
Bangalore, 560 010
www.amrutwhisky.co.uk

McDowell's
www.clubmcdowell.com

NETHERLANDS

Us Heit Distillery
Snekerstraat 43, 8701 XC
Bolsward, Friesland
www.usheitdistillery.nl

Zuidam Distillers
Smederijstraat 5, 5111 PT Baarle
Nassau
www.zuidam-distillers.com

NEW ZEALAND

The Southern Distilling Company
www.hokonuiwhisky.com

NORWAY

Buran Norsk Whisky A/S
burnors@online.no

PAKISTAN

Murree
National Park Road
P.O.Box No. 13

Postcard for **Stranahan's**
Colorado Whiskey

Rawalpindi
www.murreebrewery.com

PERU

Chilca Vid Sac
Cesar Fontana Balaguer
Los Colibries 150
Lima 27, Peru
cfontana@telefonica.net.pe

SOUTH AFRICA

James Sedgwick Distillery
Aan-de-Wagenweg
Stellenbosch 7600
www.distell.co.za

Drayman's Distillery
PO Box 1648
Silverton, Pretoria 0127
www.draymans.com

SPAIN

DYC (Distilerias y Crianza del Whisky)
Mateo Inurria 15, 28036 Madrid
www.dyc.es, www.beamglobal.com

SWEDEN

Box Destilleri
Box Kraftverk 140,
87296 Bjartra
www.boxdestillerie.se

Gotland Distillery
Sockerbruket, 622 54 Romakloster
Gotland
www.gotlandwhisky.se

Grythyttan Whisky
Nora Destilleri AB, Storg 2, 713 31
Nora
Vastmanland
www.grythyttanwhisky.com

Mackmyra Svensk Whisky, Valbo
Hantverkargatan 5, Hus 5, 112 21
Stockholm
www.mackmyra.se

Spirit of Hven
www.hven.com

SWITZERLAND

Bauernhof
Edi Bieri, Talacher, 6340 Baar
Baar, Zug
www.swissky.co

Brennerei Hagen
Destillerie V.U. Hagen Ruhli seayard
8536 Huttwilen
www.distillerie-hagen.ch

Burgdorfer Gasthausbrauerei
Wynigenstrasse 13
P.O. Box 1085,
3401 Castle Village
www.burgdorferbier.ch

Label for **Hazelnut Espresso Liqueur** by **Bendistillery** in Bend, Oregon

Maison Les Vignettes—Swhisky
Copainrative Lap'Tou,
c/o Maison Les Vignettes, Les
Vignettes 6
1957 Ardon, Valais, Switzerland
www.swhisky.ch

Spezialitätenbrennerei Zürcher
+41 (0) 32,331 85 83

Whisky Brennerei Holle
Hollen 52
4426 Lauwil
www.single-malt.ch, www.swiss-whisky.ch

Whisky Castle
Käsers Schloss AG
Schlosstrasse 17,
CH- 5077 Elfingen, Aargau
www.whisky-castle.com

TAIWAN

King Car Whisky Distillery
230, Roosevelt Road, Sec. 3, Taipei
www.kavalanwhisky.com

TURKEY

Tekel
Abide-I Hurriyet Cad.
No:285 Bolkan Center B Blok
34381 Istanbul
www.mey.com.tr

UNITED STATES

45th Parellel Spirits
1570 Madison Avenue
New Richmond, WI 54017
45thparallelspirits.com

Alltech's Lexington Brewing &
Distilling Co.
401 Cross Street
Lexington, KY 40508
www.kentuckyale.com

Anchor Distilling
1705 Mariposa Street
San Francisco, CA 94107
anchorbrewing.com

Ancient City Distilling
4041 Pine Run Circle
St. Augustine, FL 32086
(under construction)
Wksmith@aug.com

Artisan Spirits
1227 SE Stark Street
Portland, OR 97214
artisan-spirits.com

Balcones Distilling
3209 Maple Avenue
Waco, TX 76707
Balconesdistilling.com

Ballast Point Spirits
10051 Old Grove Road, Suite B
San Diego, CA 92131
ballastpoint.com

Bardenay
610 Grove Street
Boise, ID 83702
bardenay.com

Barrel House Distilling Co.
1200 Manchester Street, Building 9
Lexington, KY 40504
barrelhousedistillery.com

Bear and Eagle Products
1425 E. Borchard Street
Santa Ana, CA 92705
beareagle.com

Belmont Farms
13490 Cedar Run Road
Culpepper, VA 22701
virginiamoonshine.com

Bendistillery
1470 NE 1st Street, #800
Bend, OR 97701
bendistillery.com

Berkshire Mountain Distillers
1640 Home Road
Great Barrington, MA 01230
CTWeld@aol.com

Black Star Farms
10844 E. Revold Road
Suttons Bay, MI 49682
blackstarfarms.com

Blackwater Distilling
137 Log Canoe Circle
Stevensville, MD 21666
blackwaterdistilling@gmail.com

Brandy Peak
18526 Tetley Road
Brookings, OR 97415
brandypeak.com

Label for **Black River Gin** *by* **Sweetgrass Farm Winery and Distillery**

C&C Shine
425 Alta Street, Building 15
Gonzales, CA 93926
craigpakish@sbcglobal.net

Captain's Applejack Distillery
1 Laird Road
Scobeyville, NJ 07724
lairdandcompany.com

Cascade Peak Spirits
Box 1198
Ashland, OR 97520
cascadepeakspirits.com

Castle Spirits
18 Quickway Road # 201
Monroe, NY 10950
cspirits@juno.com

Cedar Ridge Distillery
501 7th SE Avenue, Suite B
Cedar Rapids, IA 52401
www.crwine.com

Celebration Distillation
2815 Frenchman Street
New Orleans, LA 70122
neworleansrum.com

Chateau Chantal Distillery
15900 Rue de Vin
Traverse City, MI 49686
chateauchantal.com

Clear Creek Distillery
2389 NW Wilson
Portland, OR 97210
clearcreekdistillery.com

Colorado Gold Distillery
1290 S. Grand Mesa Drive
Cedaredge, CO 81413
coloradogolddistillery.com

Colorado Pure Distillery
5609 W 6th Avenue, Unit C
Denver, CO 80214
coloradopuredistilling.com

Connecticut Valley Distillers
148 Forest Street
Manchester, CT 06040
cvdjordona@aol.com

Copper Fox Distillery
9 River Lane
Sperryville, VA 22740
copperfox.biz

Delaware Phoenix Distillery
144 Delaware Street, Box 245
Walton, NY 13856
www.delawarephoenix.com

Distillery 209
Pier 50 Shed B, Mailbox 9
Terry A. Francois Boulevard
San Francisco, CA 94158
distillery209.com

Dogfish Head Brewery & Distillery
320 Rehoboth Avenue
Rehoboth Beach, DE 19971
dogfish.com

Dolmen Distilling
Box 732
McMinnville, OR 97128
Johansena86@hotmail.com

Domaine Charbay
4001 Spring Mountain Road
St. Helena, CA 94574
charbay.com

Don Quixote Distillery
236 Rio Bravo
Los Alamos, NM 87544
dqdistillery.com

Drum Circle Distilling
2212 Industrial Boulevard
Sarasota, FL 34234
(under construction)
troy@midnightgpassrum.com

Dry Fly Distilling
1003 E. Trent #200
Spokane, WA 99202
dryflydistilling.com

Dynamic Alambic Artisan Distillery
Burle W. Figgins Jr.
Post Office Box 5066
George, Washington 98824
bwfiggins@gmail.com

Empire Winery & Distillery
11807 Little Road
New Port Richey, FL 34654
empirewineryanddistillery.com

Essential Spirits
144-A South Whisman Road
Mountain View, CA 94040
essentialspirits.com

Fat Dog Spirits
3212 North 40th Street
Tampa, FL 33605
ncarbone@pccap.com

Finger Lakes Distilling
4676 NYS Route 414
Elmira, NY 14905
fingerlakesdistilling.com

Fiore Winery & Distillery
3026 Whiteford Road
Pylesville, MD 21132
www.fiorewinery.com

*Detail from a bottle of **General John Stark Vodka** from **Flag Hill Distillery***

Flag Hill Farm
PO Box 31
Vershire, VT 05079
flaghillfarm.com

Forks of Cheat Distillery
2811 Stewartstown Road
Morgantown, WV 26508
thebigdeal@msn.com

Four Roses Distillery
1224 Bonds Mill Road
Lawrenceburg, KY 40342
fourroses.us

Garrison Brothers Distillery
Box 5932
Austin, TX 78763
garrisonbros.com

Germain-Robin
Hubert Germain-Robin
P.O. Box 1059
Ukiah, CA 95482
germain-robin.com

Golden Hill Distillery
123 Black Rock, Box 504
Redding Ridge, CT 06876
wbrucel@yahoo.com

Graham Barnes Distilling
13011 DeBarr Drive
Austin, TX 78729
treatyoakrum.com

Grand Traverse Distillery
781 Industrial Circle, Suite 5
Traverse City, MI 49686
grandtraversedistillery.com

Great Lakes Distillery
616 West Virginia Street
Milwaukee, WI 53204
greatlakesdistillery.com

Green Mountain Distillers
192 Thomas Lane
Stowe, VT 05672
greenmountaindistillers.com

Haleakala Distillery
530A Kealaloa Avenue
Maui, HI 96768
haleakaladistillers.com

Harvest Spirits
3074 US Route 9
Valatie, NY 12184
harvestspirits.com

Hawj Brother's Distillery
1841 Josephene Way
Yuba City, CA 95993
rinna1899@comcast.net

Heartland Distillers
9402 Uptown Drive, Suite 1000
Indianapolis, IN 46256
heartlanddistillers.com

Heaven Hill Distilleries, Inc.
1064 Loretto Road
Bardstown, KY 40004
heaven-hill.com

Hidden Marsh Distillery
2981 Auburn Road
Seneca Falls, NY 13148
montezumawinery.com

High Plains Distilling
1700 Rooks Road
Atchison, KS 66002
highplainsinc.com

High Spirits Distilling
15 N. Agassiz Street
Flagstaff, AZ 86001
arizonahighspirits.com

High West Distillery
703 Park Avenue
Park City, UT 84060
highwestdistillery.com

Highball Distillery
610 SE 10th Avenue
Portland, OR 97214
highballdistillery.blogspot.com

House Spirits Distillery
2025 SE 7th Avenue
Portland, OR 97214
medoyeff.com

Hubbard's Brandy House
12147 Corey Lake Road
Three Rivers, MI 49093
coreylakeorchards.com

Huber Starlight Distilery
19816 Huber Road
Borden, IN 47106
starlightdistillery.com

Indio Spirits
7110 SW Fir Loop STE 240
Portland, OR 97223
indiospirits.com

True North Vodka and
Cherry Flavored Vodka by
Grand Traverse Distillery

Integrity Spirits
909 SE Yamill Street
Portland, OR 97214
integrityspirits.com

Isaiah Morgan Distillery
45 Winery Lane
Summersville, WV 26651
kirkwood-wine.com

Island Investments & Enterprises Ltd.
914 Anglers Way
Jupiter, FL 33458
buccoobay@juno.com

Jepson Vineyards
10400 S. Highway 101
Hopland, CA 95449
www.jepsonwine.com

Keystone Distillery
120 East Baltimore Pike
Media, PA 19063
keystonedistillery@mac.com

Knapp Vineyards
2770 County Road 128
Romulus, NY 14541
knappwine.com

Koenig Distillery & Winery
20928 Grape Lane
Caldwell, ID 83607
koenigdistillery.com

Kolani Distillers
500 Balwin Avenue
Paia, HI 96779
kolanidistillers.com

Lake Placid Spirits
Box 227
Lake Placid, NY 12946
lakeplacidspirits.com

Leopold Brothers
4950 Nome Street, Unit E
Denver, CO 80239
leopoldbros.com

Liquid Ventures
818 SW 3rd Avenue, Suite 281
Portland, OR 97204
liquidvodka.com

Local Color Brewery
42705 Grand River Avenue
Novi, MI 48375
localcolor.com

Long Island Spirits
2182 Sound Avenue
Baiting Hollow, NY 11933
lispirits.com

Maine Distilleries
437 Route One
Freeport, ME 04032
coldrivervodka.com

Mancos Valley Distillery
Ian James
116 N. Main Street
Mancos, CO 81328

McMenamins Edgefield Distillery
2126 SW Halsey Street
Troutdale, OR 97060
mcmenamins.com

Michigan Brewing Company
1093 Highview Drive
Webberville, MI 48892
www.michiganbrewing.com

Modern Spirits
168 W. Pomona Avenue
Monrovia, CA 91016
modernspiritsvodka.com

Montanya Distilling Co.
1332 Notorious Blair Street
Silverton, CO 81433
montanyadistillers.com

Mosby Winery
9496 Santa Rosa Road
Buellton, CA 93427
mosbywines.com

Mt. St. Helen's Spirits
Box 728
Amboy, WA 98601
pacifier.com

Mystic Mountain Distillery
11505 Valley Road
Larkspur, CO 80118
mysticmtnspirits.com

Nashoba Distillery
100 Wattaquadock Hill Road
Bolton, MA 01740
nashobawinery.com

New Deal Distillery
1311 SE Main Street
Portland, OR 97214
newdealdistillery.com

American Single Malt Vodka in 80° and 100° proof from Stillwater Spirits

New Holland Brewing & Distilling
66 East 8th street
Holland, MI 49423
newhollandbrew.com

Newport Distilling Company
Oliphant Lane, Unit 3
Middletown, RI 02842
newportstorm.com

North Shore Distillery
Box 279
Lake Bluff, IL 60044
northshoredistillery.com

Northern Maine Distilling Company
66 Industrial Drive, Suite J
Houlton, ME 04730
twenty2vodka.com

Osocalis Distillery
5579 Old San Jose Road
Soquel, CA 95073
osocalis.com

Pacific Distillery
18808 142nd Avenue NE, #4B
Woodinville, WA 98072
pacificdistillery.com

Parched Group
310 Stockton Street
Richmond, VA 23235
cirrusvodka.com

Peach Street Distillers
144 S. Kluge Street, Building 2
Palisade, CO 81526
peachstreetdistillers.com

Peak Spirtis
26567 North Road
Hotchkiss, CO 81419
peakspirits.com

Philadelphia Distilling
12285 McNulty Road, #105
Philadelphia, PA 19154
philadelphiadistilling.com

Piedmont Distillers
203 East Murphy Street
Madison, NC 27025
piedmontdistillers.com

Pioneer Spirits
2290 Ivy Street, #150
Chico, CA 95928
pioneerspirits.com

Prichards' Distillery
11 Kelso Smithland Road
Kelso, TN 37348
prichardsdistillery.com

Railean Distillers
111 Pelican Court
League City, TX 77573
railean.com

Ransom Spirits
745 NE 5th Street
McMinnville, OR 97128
ransomspirits.com

Rogue Distillery
1339 NW Flanders
Portland, OR 97209
www.rogue.com

RoughStock Distillery
705 Osterman Drive, Suite C
Bozeman, MT 59715
montanawhiskey.com

Round Barn Distillery
10983 Hills Road
Baroda, MI 49101
roundbarnwinery.com

Roundhouse Spirits
3215 Foundry Place, #104
Boulder, CO 80301
roundhousespirits.com

Ryan & Wood Distilleries
15 Great Republic Drive, U-2
Gloucester, MA 01930
ryanandwood.com

San Luis Spirits
Box 310
Dripping Springs, TX 78620
drippingspringsvodka.com

Sarticious Spirits
427 Swift Street
Santa Cruz, CA 95060
sarticious.com

Bottle of **Hangar 1 Vodka** by **St. George Spirits**

Skyrocket Distillers
27315 Jefferson Avenue, Suite J18
Temecula, CA 92590
drinkjbw.com

A. Smith Bowman Distillery
One Bowman Drive
Fredericksburg, VA 22408
asmithbowman.com

Solomon Turner Co.
5900 Central Avenue
Calpella, CA 95418
solomon1@saber.net

Spirits of Maine
175 Chick Mill Road
Gouldsboro, ME 04607
bartlettwinery.com

St. George Spirits
2601 Monarch Street
Alameda, CA 94501
stgeorgespirits.com

St. James Spirits
5220 Fourth Street, Unit 17
Irvingdale, CA 91706
saintjamesspirits.com

St. Julian Winery
716 S. Kalamazoo Street
Paw Paw, MI 49079
stjulian.com

Stillwater Spirits
611 2nd Street
Petaluma, CA 94952
stillwaterspirits.com

Stoutridge Vineyard
10 Ann Kaley Lane
Marlboro, NY 12542
stoutridge.com

Stranahan's Colorado Whiskey
2405 Blake Street
Denver, CO 80205
stranahans.com

Stringer's Orchard Wild Plum Distillery
Box 191, Highway 395
New Pine Creek, OR 97635
stringersorchard.com

Sub Rosa Spirits
876 SW Alder Drive
Dundee, OR 97115
subrosaspirits.com

Swedish Hill Winery
4565 Route 414
Romulus, NY 14541
swedishhill.com

Sweetgrass Farm Winery and Distillery
347 Carrol Road
Union, ME 04862
sweetgrasswinery.com

Syntax Spirits
1409 E. Olive Court, Unit A
Fort Colins, CO 80524
syntaxspirits.com

Templeton Rye
206 East 3rd Street
Templeton, IA 51463
templetonrye.com

The Solas Distillery
17070 Wright Plaza
Omaha, NE 68130
upstreambrewing.com

Tito's
12101 Moore Road
Austin, TX 78719
titos-vodka.com

Triple Eight Disitillery
5 Bartlett Farm Road
Nantucket, MA 02584
ciscobrewers.com

Tuthilltown Spirits
14 Gristmill Lane
Gardiner, NY 12525
tuthilltown.com

Uncle John's Fruit House
8614 N. U.S. 127
St. Johns, MI 48879
ujcidermill.com

Vermont Spirits
PO Box 272
St. Johnsbury, VT 05819
vermontspirits.com

Warwick Valley Distillery
114 Little York Road
Warwick, NY 10990
wvwinery.com

West Virginia Distilling
1380 Fenwick Avenue
Morgantown, WV 26505
mountainmoonshine.com

Tito Beveridge of Tito's Handmade Vodka

Westford Hill Distillers
196 Chatey Road
Ashford, CT 06278
westfordhill.com

Woodstone Creek
3641 Newton Avenue
Cincinnati, OH 45207
woodstonecreek.com

Wyoming Whiskey
300 North Nelso
Kirby, WY 82430
stevewydistillery1@rtconnect.net

Yahara Bay Distillers
3118 Kingsley Way
Madison, WI 53713
yaharabay.com

Yellowstone Valley Brewing
2123 1st Avenue North
Billings, MT 59101
yellowstonevalleybrew.com

UNITED STATES: THE OLD GUARD

Most whiskey in the United States has been, and still is being made by long established distilleries in Kentucky and Tennessee. The Jim Beam Distillery traces its origins to the late eighteenth century, while Buffalo Trace has been in operation since the mid-nineteenth century. Today all of them welcome visitors, with hospitality centers that range from small town charm (George Dickel) to major museum impressiveness (Heaven Hill).

Beam Global (Jim Bean)
149 Happy Hollow Road, Box 160
Clermont, KY 40110
www.jimbeam.com

Buffalo Trace Distillery
1001 Wilkonson Boulevard
Frankfort, KY 40601
www.buffalotrace.com

George A. Dickel & Co.
1970 Cascade Hollow Road
Tullahoma, TN 37388
georgedickel.com

Jack Daniel's Distillery
182 Lynchburg Highway
Lynchburg, TN 37352
jackdaniels.com

Maker's Mark Distillery, Inc.
3350 Burks Spring Road
Loretto, KY 40037
makersmark.com

Tom Moore Distillery
Box 788, 1 Barton Road
Bardstown, KY 40004
bartoninc.com

Wild Turkey Distillery
1525 Tyrone Road
Lawrenceburg, KY 40324

wildturkey@qualitycustomercare.com

Woodford Reserve Distillery
7855 McCracken Pike
Versailles, KY 40383
woodfordreserve.com

INDEX

Prichard, Phil, 109, *109*, *141*, 141
Prichard's Crystal Rum, *94*
Prichard's Distillery, *42*, *94*, 99, *109*, 109, *141*, 141
Prichard's Fine Rum, *94*, 109
prohibition, 73
Prohibition Era Whiskey, *18*
Prohibition (National), 16, 18, 43, 57, 67, 74, 87, 95, 141
Puerto Rico, 92, 98
pulque, 100

Q
Quady, Andy, 71
Quady Winery, 71
Quakers, 73
Quebec, 51
Quint, Jeff, *110*

R
Ragged Mountain Rum, *97*
raspberry brandy, 90
Raspberry Liqueur, *159*
recipe books, 13
recipes (cocktails), 61, 70, 78, 91, 97, 105
rectification, 25, 26, 34, 51, 67, 68, 75–76
Red Hook, Brooklyn, 71
redistillation. *See* rectification
reflux, 29, 35
reflux columns, 25
regional flavors, 51
regulation, 14–15
Rehorst, Guy, *76*
Reinhold, Frank, *134*, 134
Remy Martin, 88
Rendezvous Rye Whiskey, *44*
Repeal, 43, 57, 67, 74, 87
resources, 143–153
Revere, Paul, 73
Reynolds, Burt, 17
Rhine River, 90
Rhode Island, 136
rhum, 96, 98
rhum agricole, 98
rhum industriel, 98
rhum vieux, 98
RMS, 87–88
Rocky Mountain Blackberry, 107
Rogue Distillery, 99, *99*, *121*, 121
Rogue Distillery and Ale House, *75*, *95*
roots, 107
Rosolis Ziolowy Gorzki, *107*
rotgut, 16, 25
Rothes, Scotland, 58
rum, 30, 41, 73, 79, 92, *92*, 93–99, 109
  aged rum, 96, 97
  Asian, 99
  Australian, 99
  basis of, 96
  Blanco, 92
  in the British colonies, 93, 94–95
  in Canada, 99
  Caribbean, 98
  in Central America, 98–99
  column stills and, 97
  Cuban, 98
  dark, 95
  Demerara, 92, 96, 98
  distillation of, 97
  distilling timeline, 57
  European, 95–96, 99
  Filipino, 99
  golden, 95
  Guyanan, 92, 96, 98
  Haitian, 98
  history of, 93–96
  increasing popularity of, 96
  inlander rum, 99
  Jamaican, 96, 98, 99
  in Martinique, 96, 98

North American, 99
pot stills and, 97
Puerto Rican, 92, 98
by region, 98–99
resources on, 148–149
rum verschnitt, 99
South American, 98–99
spiced, 95
styles of, 95
in the UK, 99
in the US, 95, 99, 141–143
white, 95, 96
Rum and Coke, 97
rumbullion, 94
rum cocktails, 97
rummagers, 30
rum verschnitt, 99
Rupf, Jorg, *112*, 112
Russell, Jimmy, 71
Russia, 13, 65, 68–69
Russian vodka, 68–69
Rusty Nail, 61
Ryan, Bob, *94*
Ryan, Brett, 136, *136*
Ryan and Wood Distilleries, *94*
rye, 41, 68, 69
rye mash, 68
rye whiskey, 41, 43, 44–45, 48, 51

S
Sagatiba Pura Cachaça, *98*
sambuca, 107
San Francisco, California, 114
San Francisco International Wine and Spirits Competition, 140
San Francisco Wine and Spirits Competition, 137
San Luis Potosí, Mexico, 101
Santa Cruz Mountains, 88, *117*, 117
Sarticious Gin, 78
Sarticious Spirits, 78
Sauvignon blanc vines, *116*, 116
Sauza family, 101
Saveur magazine, 137
Sazerac, 61
Sazerac Rye Whiskey, *61*
Scandinavia, 65, 107. *See also specific nations*
schnapps, 30, 34, 92, 107
Scotch whisky, 40, 53, 58, 60
  basis of, 60
  blended, 54, 57
  distillation of, 60
  grain whisky, *59*, 60
  history of, 53, 55–56
  malt whisky, 28, 30, 54, 55, 60
  by region, 60
  resources on, 152–153
  single malts, *59*
  vatted malt, *59*
Scotland, 13, 40, 41, 53, 56, 60
Scottish Highlands, 55, 58, 60
screech, 99
Screwdriver, 70
sealed pots, 13
separation, 24–25, 29, 34
Sercial brandy, 88
Settles, Kevin, *125*, 125
Sex on the Beach, 70
sheepskin, 12
sherry, 69
shochu, 58
siddqui, 23
Sidecar, 91
Sienkiewicz, Kieran, *121*, 121
sieve trays, 33
sight glasses, 25–26
Sinedrius, Libya, 13
single barrel bourbon, 48
single malts, 54, *59*
single malt Scotch whisky, *59*

single-run distillation, 38
Skye, Scotland, 60
Skyrocket Distillers, 105, *115*, 115
"slavery triangle", 95
Slavs, 65
slivovitz, 23, 91
sljiva plums, 91
sloe gin, 74
small batch bourbon, 48
Smirnoff, 67
Smothers, LeNell, 71, *71*
Snake River Stampede Blended Canadian Whisky, *46*
solera method, 84–85, 86, 87
sour mashes, 42, 52
"sour mash" grain conversion technique, 42
the South, 42–43, 141–143. *See also specific states*
South Africa, 88
South America, 88, 98–99
South Carolina, 67
Southern Comfort, 107
Soviet Union, 65
Spain, 13, 69, 84–86
Spanish colonies, 93, 100–101
Spanish explorers, 93, 100
Speyside, Scotland, 60
spiced rum, 95
spices, 73, 75
Spicy Ginger, *107*
spirits, resources on, 145–147
Spirits Journal, 137
Spirits of Maine Distilleries, 138, *138*
spirit stills, 37
Spruce Gin, *75*
Stanford, Leland, 87
steam jackets, 30, 33
St. George Spirits, 11, 88, 105, 108, *108*, 112, *112*, *148*
stills, 12, *103*, *111*, 113, *113*
  alambic, *35*, 115, *115*, 117, *117*, 120, *120*
  batch, 31
  blueprint of, *14*, *22*, *23*
  Chavlignac Prulho brandy, 114, *114*, 116, *116*, *117*, 117
  column, *22*
  continuous-run column, 27, 31, *39*
  craft whiskey, *28*
  design of, 13–14, 25–26, 27–35, *28*
  double-jacketed steam-water system, 25
  French Charentais alambic, 27, *32*, 32–33, 35
  glass, 126, *126*
  gooseneck, 27, 28–30, *29*, *30*, *140*
  high-separation, 25, 26, 31
  Holstein, 112, *112*
  lower-separation, 32
  mash, 143
  moonshine, *16*, 27
  optional components, 35
  parts of, 25–26, *27*
  personal, 16
  physics of, 21
  portable, 84, *84*
  pot, *22*, *23*, *26*, 27, *33–35*, 33–35, *38*, 115, *115*
  spirit, *22*
  traveling, 15
  vendome, *114*, 114, 141, *141*
Stillwater Spirits, 114, *114*
Stinger, 91
stirring paddle, *48*
St. James Spirits, *50*, 105
St. Julian, 91
Stoutridge Vineyard, *38*
straight whiskey, 52
Stranahan, George, *127*
Stranahan's Colorado Whiskey, *40*, *127*, 127, *151*, *160*
Stringer's Orchard Wild Plum Winery & Distillery, *23*, *123*, 123

About the Contributors

ALTHOUGH it may seem that Alan Dikty wrote every word in this book, and that Bill Owens took every photograph, that is not the case. The following collection of the usual suspects had a hand in it all, for which we are very grateful.

Andrew Faulkner

Andrew Faulkner didn't drink at all in high school, but he did photograph and learned much from his friend Ansel Adams. He was introduced to the joy of liquor in his early twenties, by an alcoholic girlfriend. His drinking education continued through his thirties, playing loud music and dealing with various band members' chemical dependencies. He was the photography editor of the *Warsaw Business Journal*, and during four Polish winters, he did serious research into Eastern European distillates, or research into serious Eastern European distillates. The photography and drinking came together when he met Bill Owens and started working for the American Distilling Institute. He has tasted most of the liquors pictured in this book.

Mike McCaw

Mike McCaw is a cofounder and director of the Amphora Society and the coauthor of *The Compleat Distiller*, widely recognized as the primary technical publication concerning all aspects of small-scale distillation. McCaw now spends most of his time consulting with start-up craft and microdistillers and designing and building equipment for their operations. His current research is on further increasing the efficiency and lowering the carbon and water footprints of distilling processes. A book is in preparation detailing some of these techniques. He is working to create a series of hands-on workshops for aspiring distillers, and also on stirring up grassroots interest in legalization of private, noncommercial distillation in the United States.

Matthew B. Rowley

Matthew Rowley is an advertising executive, former museum curator, and past board member of the Southern Foodway Alliance. He has traveled extensively in search of amateur and craft distillers to uncover local liquor and, when possible, promote those who make it.

He has spoken on distilling and cocktail culture for universities, radio, television, and the annual Tales of Cocktail in New Orleans. His essays and recipes have been published by the University of North Carolina Press, the University of Georgia Press, Simon & Schuster, the Taunton Press, Lark Books, and others. He has consulted on distilling-related broadcasts for the FOX network and the National Geographic Channel in the United States and RTE in Ireland.

Rowley lives in San Diego, California, where he maintains a two-thousand-volume culinary library open to chefs, bartenders, distillers, historians, journalists, and students. He is the author of *Moonshine!* (2007), a small batch distilling history/practicum for novices and publishes Rowley's Whiskey Forge (www.whiskey forge.com), a blog devoted to the history and practice of distilling, mixology, and good eats.

Ian Smiley

Ian Smiley, BSc, is a research distiller and the author of the book *Making Pure Corn Whiskey*, an Amphora Society publication, and the owner of Smiley's Home Distilling at www.home-distilling. com, a Web store dedicated to home and laboratory distillers. He has been exploring small-scale beverage-alcohol distillation all his adult life, and he is a card-carrying member of the American Distilling Institute (ADI). He's written articles for their magazine, *The American Distiller*, and was a major contributor to the recently published ADI book, *Craft Whiskey Distilling*. He is now part owner of a whiskey distillery in China, L.S. Moonshine, which is currently producing a corn whiskey white dog to satisfy the Chinese people's curiosity for traditional American moonshine. L.S. Moonshine has other spirits planned for the Chinese market. In the future, Smiley plans to write books on making schnapps, brandy, and rum, and to continue his activities in commercial artisan distilling. He lives in Nepean, Ontario, Canada.

MAX WAXMAN

Max Waxman is the author of *Chasing the White Dog: An Amateur Outlaw's Adventures in the Moonshine Trade*, which will be published by Simon and Schuster in early 2010. His book *Race Day: A Spot on the Rail with Max Watman* (Ivan R. Dee) was called "a great tribute to American thoroughbred racing" and was an Editors' Choice in the *New York Times Book Review*.

He was the horse racing correspondent for the *New York Sun*, and wrote frequently on books, music, food, and drink for their Arts & Letters pages. He has written for the *New York Times*, the *New York Times Book Review*, *Forbes FYI*, *The Wall Street Journal*, *Fortune Small Business*, *Gourmet*, and *Parnassus*.

He was raised in the mountains of Virginia, and has worked as a cook, a farmer, a silversmith, a tutor, a greenskeeper, and a warehouseman. For a short time he taught goat milking. He was educated at many schools, and managed to graduate from Virginia Commonwealth University and Columbia University.

In 2008, Waxman was awarded a National Endowment for the Arts literary fellowship.

ACKNOWLEDGMENTS

EARLIER VERSIONS of some of the text in this book previously appeared in various publications of the Beverage Testing Institute, and it is used here with the permission of BTI director **Jerald O'Kennard**, and our grateful thanks.

Bill Owens cannot draw worth a damn, so we had **Catherine Ryan** redo his primitive sketches in a much more polished manner. They look great.

Amber Hasselbring serves as Bill's assistant and caregiver. Whatever he is paying her, it is not enough. The woman is a saint.

Mixing a proper drink is truly an art, and **Mark Gruber** of Southern Wine & Spirits, Illinois, confirmed his artistic talent by reviewing and correcting our mixed drink recipes as needed. The man even writes tasty.

ABOUT THE AUTHORS

Bill Owens and Alan Dikty

ALAN S. DIKTY is the author of *The Buying Guide to Spirits* and numerous articles on distilling and brewing. In his spare time he manages Allied Beverage Tanks, Inc., a company that builds craft breweries and distilleries. His current choice for a desert island dram is either Macallan 18 Year Old Scotch Whisky or Rittenhouse 23 Year Old Rye Whiskey, but he is open to alternatives.

BILL OWENS, when he was not busy being an award-winning photographer or the founder of the brewpub industry in the United States, somehow also found the time to be the author of an assortment of books and pamphlets on brewery and distillery operations, including, most recently, *Craft Whiskey Distilling*, published by the ADI. In his spare time he tries his best to avoid personal responsibilities. www.distilling.com